DESTINATION "GUSTAV"

DESTINATION "GUSTAV"

A Wartime Journey

by

Gilbert Van Grieken

First published 1992

Made and printed in Great Britain by The Guernsey Press Co. Ltd, Guernsey, Channel Islands.

ISBN 0-902550-47-0

CONTENTS

LIST OF ILLUSTRATIONS

FOREWORD

I first met Gisbertus Van Grieken in the summer of 1942 whilst working for the Guernsey Civil Service at St Peter Port Weighbridge. He asked me for a drink of water and I was able to provide him with a cup of coffee from my thermos flask.

From that time on we became friends and I got to know the Dutch boys who, like Gis (or Gilbert as he is now known), were brought to Guernsey by the Organisation Todt and eventually married Guernsey girls — Piet Vermeulen, Frans de Pee, Bill Spoelstra, Jaap Jonkmans — to name a few.

In this narrative a certain Mijnheer Mann is mentioned, (he is also mentioned in *Prey of an Eagle* by K. M. Bachmann). When I met him I was under the impression that he was concerned with the wellbeing and welfare of the Dutch workers. However, he was so surprised to come across a Dutch speaking Guernseyman that he presented me with a very large Dutch/English dictionary, which I use to this day.

Gilbert Van Grieken's story is one he felt had to be told — an account of one of the many who were compelled to do forced labour by the occupying German forces. They suffered many deprivations, faced many uncertainties but maintained the courage necessary for survival.

G. P. Lowe, Guernsey, 21 April 1987.

Studio portrait of Gilbert Van Grieken — 1940

INTRODUCTION

In the spring of 1940 Adolf Hitler, Führer of the German Third Reich, unleashed the military might of Germany against the nations of Western Europe. Within a space of two months German forces were in military occupation of Europe from the Arctic Circle to the Atlantic Ocean. World War II, which had been declared seven months earlier and had been named the 'Phoney War', started in earnest.

The next five years were to be years of misery for millions of people across Europe. The fate of those slaughtered in great battles or exterminated in the notorious gas chambers of the concentration camps set up by the Nazis to effect Hitler's 'final solution' of his so-called Jewish problem has been well documented and noted by history. But there were millions more whose lives were to be savagely torn apart during these years. Forcibly separated from family and friends they were the unseen victims of the Nazi scourge whose sufferings, although less dramatic than that of those who made the headlines, were nevertheless real to them.

They were like the small creatures whose fate goes unnoticed when a volcano erupts. They suffer as well but they are too many, and lack public importance, for much notice to be taken of each one.

This is the story of just one victim of the tide of events which was to engulf Europe between 1940 and 1945. The story of this Dutchman is typical of the millions who became displaced persons in the cause of the German war machine. It is told to remember those countless innocent victims of man's mindless devotion to the destruction of his neighbours in war, victims whose names are only recorded in archives buried in some dusty vault.

The little people are still suffering today the consequences of wars, many small and some among brothers. They are the victims of the arms salesmen who jet around the world peddling death and mutilation to any who will buy their machines of destruction.

The casualties of these many wars, still being fought nearly half a century after the global conflict ended in the terrible fireballs which engulfed the Japanese towns of Hiroshima and Nagasaki, should not be overlooked. They are as important to the history of man as the much publicised victims of the Nazi holocaust.

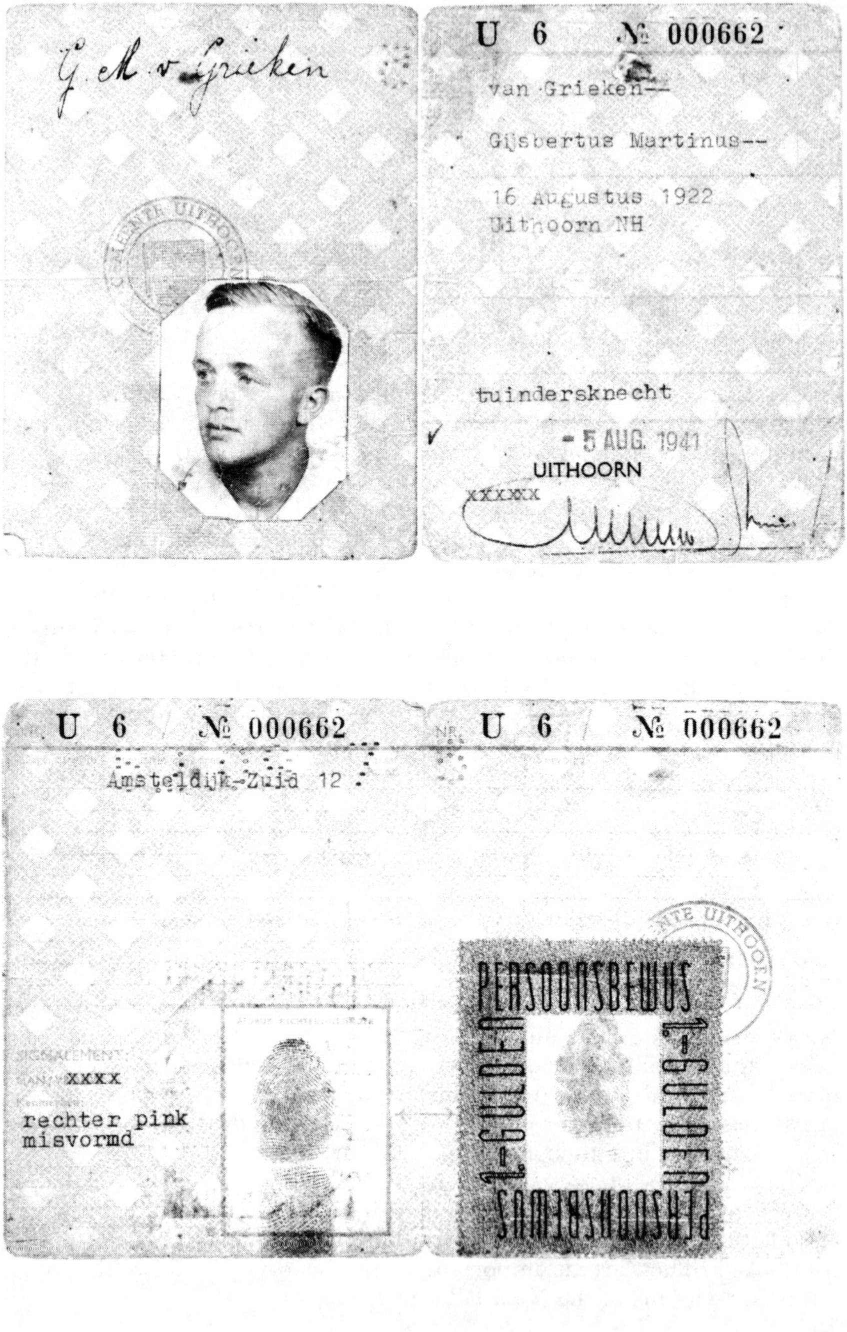

Dutch Identity Card — issued 1941

Chapter 1

THE IMPOSSIBLE HAPPENS

After a long and bitterly cold winter the people of Northwest Europe faced the spring of 1940 in a mood of waiting and watching. The belligerent countries, Germany, Britain and France had spent the past few months indulging in a propaganda war, hurling invective at each other. Apart from a few naval actions, none approaching the scale of the naval battles of the Great War, the war seemed more of an inconvenience than a threat to life and limb.

The neutral countries, Norway, Denmark, Holland, Belgium and Luxemburg waited and wondered when the belligerents would make their move. For the Dutch and Belgians, particularly, the waiting was tense as they remembered the events of 1914-18, but all they could do was to watch, wait and prepare for the onslaught they felt sure would come.

Life for the people of the neutral countries at this time was far from normal. Although they had solemnly declared their neutrality and announced their intention of maintaining normal and friendly relations with all the nations at war, the effect of the Allied naval blockade of European ports seriously affected the normal trading patterns. Shipping belonging to the neutral nations was stopped and searched for any cargo considered to be destined for Germany. Such cargoes were seized to prevent the neutral countries providing Germany with food or strategic raw materials by way of trade.

The restrictions on normal trade caused by the blockade badly damaged the peacetime economies of the neutral countries and, in addition, they were forced to, at least partially, mobilise their armed forces. In the case of Holland and Belgium huge sums of money had to be spent on building lines of defence. All of Europe was on a war footing during those bright spring days with their promise of a long warm summer.

The first blow fell on 9 April, 1940 when German forces overran Denmark in one day and continued northward to occupy Norway. Although the Norwegians, with some British assistance, put up a spirited resistance their efforts were fruitless. Not only was there a strong pro-Nazi element in Norway, led by the notorious Quisling, but the sheer weight of the German invasion force quickly overwhelmed the smaller, and less prepared, Norwegian army and air force.

In the west, Holland and Belgium still waited. Neither country had any fear of Allied aggression against their frontiers and the costly preparations they had been forced to make to defend their independence were inspired entirely by fear of German actions and the evidence of Germany's total disregard for international law or declarations of neutrality.

With Allied armies massed on their borders, both Holland and Belgium prepared defensive positions by which they hoped their own forces could withstand a German attack until help could reach them from the Allies. In Holland the plan of defence lay largely in the ability of the Dutch to flood large areas of land thus preventing the movement of the German armoured columns expected to spearhead the attack. In Belgium the defences were along the lines of canals, very similar to those used in 1914.

It was this 1914 thinking which was to prove the undoing of not only Holland and Belgium but also the British and French. The Allies were convinced that the German attack, when in came, would follow the very nearly successful Schlieffen Plan used by the Kaiser in the earlier war. This plan called for a German attack through Belgium to punch holes in the Allied lines then for the German armies to swing south, in a series of concentric circles, to encircle the Allied armies and to capture Paris.

The Germans had other ideas. The Allied naval blockade was starving their people of food and their war machine of essential materials. What they needed more than anything was ports, as many as they could capture, to break the stranglehold the Allies had on the North Sea ports. This is what they went for.

The attack came on 10 May 1940 when, at 2.30 in the morning, the Germans attacked the neutral countries with a massive weight of air power. Thousands of parachute troops, a form of military advance never seen before and on a scale never imagined by the defenders of the Low Countries, were dropped behind the defence lines prepared. The Dutch and Belgian forces found themselves with the enemy both in front and behind them. They were quickly routed. The objectives of the parachute troops were to secure the routes by which the armoured columns could reach their selected destinations, the Channel ports. To make it clear that resistance was useless the Germans backed up the advance of their troops with heavy bombing raids against major towns. Two square miles of Rotterdam were flattened in a single raid lasting a bare 30 minutes.

So fast was the speed, and so unexpected the direction, of the attack that neither Holland or Belgium had time to reorganise their defences nor the Allies to move forward to their aid. The superior German forces totally destroyed Dutch resistance to their advance by 14 May.

The Belgians surrendered on 27 May and the French on 22 June. The entire coast of Europe from northern Norway to the French/Spanish frontier was under the control of Germany by the end of June 1940.

The occupation of Holland had been carried out with such terrifying speed and efficiency that the inhabitants couldn't believe what had happened. It was impossible their country had been overrun so soon. But the impossible had happened as Gilbert Van Grieken was to learn only too soon.

On 10 May, Van Grieken, then 17-years old and employed by a building contractor as an apprentice carpenter, went to his place of work at the new, nearly completed, railway station of Amstel (Amsterdam South). He did not have far to travel from the family home on Mollukkenstraat, where they had just moved to from Borgerstraat, but he was a little apprehensive as he cycled along since only a week earlier he had been stopped by a policeman for riding his bicycle in the early morning darkness without lights. This had resulted in him being taken to the police station where, because he was carrying no means of identification, he had been detained for three hours while the police checked his story and confirmed he was a Dutch citizen. In the nervous days of 1940 nobody was taken on trust.

Knowing nothing of the events of the past few hours he was surprised, when he reached his destination, to find a small crowd standing in front of the station. Rumours abounded. The Germans had landed parachute troops disguised as priests and nuns. They were going to bomb every town into rubble. The German army had drowned when the dykes were opened. Nobody really knew what was happening so they just waited and watched.

They didn't have long to wait. Very soon the first German troops appeared, moving into position to occupy important strategic installations in the town. The young Dutchman watched and wept in anger and disbelief as a woman ran across the road to hand a bunch of flowers to German soldiers.

"That bitch must be a German," was the comment of one of the crowd. She probably wasn't, as the Dutch people were to find out when they realized the worst they had feared had come to pass. They were soon to learn they were prisoners of Germany in their own country and, what was worse, their goalers were being helped by their own people.

In London, on the same day, Dutch Ministers visited Winston Churchill, then still First Lord of the Admiralty, and told him of the events in Holland. They told him of the overwhelming onslaught, made without warning, from the air and how the Dutch defence lines had been crossed by thousands of parachute troops.

The only advice Churchill could give the Dutch Ministers was to bring their Queen and government to London and he ordered a British flotilla operating off the Dutch coast to arrange the evacuation. The

Royal Navy went into action and took on board two destroyers Queen Wilhelmina, together with Prince Bernhard and Crown Princess Juliana and their five children. Also boarded were members of the Netherlands Government and around 100 officials and military personnel. At the same time several Dutch warships loaded another 3,000 men and the entire merchant navy in Dutch ports was ordered to England.

Queen Wilhelmina authorised the Dutch Commander in Chief, General H. G. Winkelman, to take whatever action he thought necessary to avoid further bloodshed. On May 14 General Winkelman ordered his troops to cease fire but refused to capitulate to the invading forces. Holland never officially surrendered to the Germans.

No sooner had the Queen left than keen supporters of the Nazi cause emerged from the woodwork and announced their readiness to form a civil administration eager to do the bidding of the conquering armies. It took little time for the Germans to install these enthusiastic collaborators, who they had probably long before earmarked as sympathisers whose support could be relied on, in positions of authority, armed with all the powers of the law of the land, and to instruct them in the actions they must take to meet the needs of the Third Reich.

While announcing he had no intention of oppressing the "Kindred Dutch people" Hitler appointed the Austrian Nazi Party leader Dr. Seyss-Inquart as *Reichs-Kommisar* for the Netherlands. At the same time, just to make sure the "Dutch kinsmen" did as they were told, Hitler appointed a ruthless Gestapo man, SS Obergruppen-Führer Hans Rauter as *Higher SS and Police Commissioner.* Very soon the Dutch were to witness the sight of Seyss-Inquart assuring them he had no intention of "imposing on them an ideology that was unacceptable"while his colleague was busy taking into custody Dutch politicians, churchmen and trade union leaders who had failed to embrace their German conquerors with suitable enthusiasm.

Before long the Germans began to stamp their mark on Dutch life. The inhabitants of the Jewish quarter of Amsterdam, centered on the Joden Breestraat, were forced to wear the yellow Star of David and were to be progressively shipped off to the extermination camps. The Jewish quarter no longer exists as 160,000 of them perished in the holocaust. In the whole of Holland less than 20,000 survived the war. In March 1941, 500 Jewish hostages were taken away by the Germans in reprisal for the killing of one German policeman.

Following the practice enforced in the other occupied countries the German authorities in Holland ordered the requisition of all stocks of a wide range of products including foodstuffs, cattle fodder, oil products, precious and semi precious stones, gold, silver, leather and timber. Materials of every description, in short supply in Germany, were seized and transported to the Reich.

The outcome of this policy was devastation for the Dutch economy. Without materials many businesses had to close and discharge their labour on to a labour market with no need for manpower. Such was the fate of young Van Grieken. His employer was forced to close his business and discharge his employees. They were left to fare as best they could.

While Holland, and the other occupied countries which had suffered the same pillage of their food and materials stocks, had an army of unemployed labour, Germany, much of her manpower called up to form the vast armies needed to turn the Führer's grandiose plans for the Greater German Empire into action, was suffering a severe shortage of labour to man the factories producing equipment needed to support those armies, the navy and Luftwaffe. Manpower had to be found.

The solution was simple. In Holland, for example, a decree was passed requiring all unemployed men to report to the labour office to be registered for employment in Germany, or elsewhere, as directed by the German labour authorities. There was no escaping this decree as Dutch employers were forbidden to take on new employees without the prior permission of the labour office. By use of this decree the Dutch authorities had, by October 1940, provided Germany with 40,000 workers, by March 1941, this figure had risen to 90,000.

So the fates dealt with Gilbert Van Grieken. Some two months after he registered he received a notice instructing him to report to Amsterdam Central railway station for transport to Germany where he would be given employment. In the same notice were orders that he was to surrender his food ration card. Failure to obey the order, he was warned, would result in arrest by the Dutch police and compulsory transfer to the jurisdiction of the German authorities, for disposal as they wished. Having no job, no money and the prospect of no food without a ration card, he had little choice but to comply. Bidding his family goodbye, not knowing where he was going or when he would see them again, with a heavy heart he reported as instructed.

This was to be the start of five interminable years of conscript labour to be performed where and when the Germans ordered. His travels were to take him from Berlin, in the east, to La Rochelle, in the west, and finally to the Channel Island of Guernsey, then under military occupation by the German army and known to the Organisation Todt, into whose fiendishly cruel hands Van Grieken was to fall. By the codeword "Gustav", Jersey was "Jakob" and Alderney "Abel."

Chapter 2
THE JOURNEY BEGINS

Arriving at Amsterdam Central station on a bleak November day, carrying the one suitcase permitted and a supply of food to last one day as ordered, Van Grieken reported himself to the railway transport officer in charge of the special train waiting in the station to transport the Dutch *Zwangarbeiters* to Germany. He was told to board the train, where he found several hundred fellow conscript workers all wondering what was in store for them.

The train eventually left Amsterdam and, after a journey of six hours, arrived in the German capital, Berlin. The travellers knew then, at least their destination but precious little else. Disembarking from the train they were loaded into lorries and taken to what appeared to be a disused mental hospital where they were herded into a very large assembly hall and told to line up against the walls. Every now and again an enormous man, with wild staring eyes, would emerge from a side room and bark commands at the frightened Dutchmen telling them to stand still, stand where they had been told, stop talking. So strange was the appearance of this individual that the workers wondered if he wasn't one of the mental patients left over from the evacuation of the hospital.

Eventually the Dutchmen were split into small groups and ushered into another room and told the factories they had been allocated to for work. Van Grieken's group were then taken to an empty hotel in the Eichendorf Strasse and informed this was to be their permanent quarters. The next day they would be taken to their workplaces.

The next day some 20 of the workers, including Van Grieken, were taken to an AEG factory in Ackerstrasse, some 10 minutes walk from the hotel. The factory was part of AEG's instrument division and manufactured instruments, clocks, etc. for aircraft and submarines. On arrival at the factory the men were briefed about the work they were expected to do, the arrangements made for paying their wages (at a rate approximately half that paid to German workers), partly in Reichmarks to cover their living expenses and the remainder would be sent to their families in Holland. They were given food and tobacco ration cards, allowing them the same rations as German civilians, and told that after six months satisfactory service they would be allowed to return home on leave. It was explained to them they would be given one main meal each day in the factory canteen but both the meat and fat coupons on their ration cards had to be surrendered to the canteen in return for these meals. The remainder of the coupons they were free to use as they liked to buy the remainder of their food.

Berlin, in the winter of 1940/41 was a city at war but by no means downhearted. Although the peace the Germans had been sure would come after their successful conquest of nearly all Europe had not materialised, they were confident of the eventual outcome of the war.

The Berliners were well dressed, often elegant, but they were disposed to look the other way when they encountered, in the streets, the tattered and half-starved working parties from the slave labour camps or prisoners of war clad in threadbare uniforms.

There were uniforms everywhere. Uniforms of the Nazi Party, the German army, navy and air force. Todt Organisation, Corps of Nazi drivers, Hitler Youth, the League of German Maidens, police, firemen and so on. Arrogance was the order of the day and poorly dressed workers from the labour camps had to step off the footpath to let a German pass by without hindrance.

Such was the confidence of the German Government at this time that the war would be a short affair they used the supplies of food, arriving from the occupied countries in increasing quantities, to compensate the German people for the problems caused by the increasing activity of the Royal Air Force who were visiting German cities night after night to bomb factories and military installations. The rations of butter, meat, sugar, flour and eggs were increased. To a people conditioned to the concept of "Guns before butter" this was a sure sign of eventual victory and the dominance of the German nation over all Europe.

It didn't take long for the young, and very unsophisticated, Van Grieken to fall out with his German masters. One day the department manager called him and another, somewhat older, man to a window. Pointing to a pile of coal in the yard he said, "I want you to shovel all that coal slack into the wagon and report back to me when you have finished." Led by the older man, probably more used to the inevitable clash between management and labour, the two refused saying they hadn't been brought there to shovel coal and anyway they had no coats and gloves and it was bitterly cold outside. Give then some clothes to protect them from the cold and they would do it. The manager was furious and threatened the men with all manner of unpleasant fates if they refused to do his bidding. The men were adamant. No clothing, no shovelling. The manager gave up. He must have eventually got somebody else to do the job for a few days later the heap of coal had vanished. This clash with authority, which he won, may have given the young Dutchman a false impression of an easy going nature in the

German character. He was to find out differently in his next clash, this time with the German police.

The manager involved in the coal affair did not seem to hold it against the young man. He moved him to a new job working with a German girl named Helena. She was about 24 years old, blonde, of medium height and quite pretty.

Their job was to make up packages of what are known in the world of manufacturing industries as attaching parts, screws, washers, nuts and bolts as required by the assembly lines of the factory. Lists of requirements would be supplied and the young man would fill paper bags with the materials requested. These bags would be passed to the girl who marked the bags with the destination to which they were intended.

The two got on well together. The very young man who had no experience of dealing with women and the older girl, probably with a fiance or boyfriend away in some distant land, formed a sympathetic friendship but always conscious of the difference in their respective positions in the order of things. They sat on opposite sides of a table and would chat while they filled and marked the bags of parts. When the opportunity offered, and nobody was about, the young man would put his hands under the table and fondle the girl's knees. Helena clearly didn't object to this performance but it tended to slow down the rate of work to the extent the manager of the department was moved on several occasions to tell young Gilbert not to talk so much and get on with his work. On one such occasion the manager told him, "We'll never win the war at this rate, you know," but otherwise he took no notice of the mild flirtation going on between the two.

Around the beginning of 1941 Van Grieken had another conflict with German authority. He was walking around the factory seeing what was going on. He used to walk about with documents under his arm so that if anybody asked him what he was doing in a part of the factory where he was not known he would claim he had lost his way and ask to be directed back to his own department. On one such trip he met a German worker from his department who demanded that the Dutchman help him push a trolley. Van Grieken agreed to help but found himself pushing the trolley with the German walking behind offering no assistance. They came to a narrow passageway with a door and the German made to leap on the trolley to open the door to a lift but he misjudged his step and one wheel of the trolley went over his foot.

The German was furious. Cursing at the top of his voice he made a dive for the Dutchman with the intention of giving him a good thrashing. The victim of this attack tried to protect himself with his arms but somehow his fist came in contact with the German's nose, knocking off his glasses. The outraged German stepped back, picked up his glasses, and told the Dutchman he would report him for attacking a German.

Van Grieken pushed the trolley into the lift and returned to his workplace where he got on with the job of filling paper bags with parts.

Some 30 minutes later two security guards came into the department, asked his name and being given it told him to come with them. They marched off, one guard in front and the other behind, to an office where the offended German stood with two civilian policemen. His glasses, falling off during the minor scuffle, had scraped a small piece of skin off his nose, the damaged bit being covered with plaster. The German police interrogated Van Grieken as the German had complained he had been struck with a piece of metal, he thought a folded pocket knife. The Dutchman protested he had only been defending himself against a savage and unprovoked attact and he couldn't have hit the German with a pocket knife as he didn't have one. One of the policemen grabbed the accused and shook him as he was leaning against a table but, at the same time, turned to the complaining German and told him he was making a lot of fuss about a trivial matter. However, since the incident had been reported, they would have to follow the recognised procedure for such complaints. Van Grieken was sent back to work with a strong warning not to fight again with a German *Arbeitskamerad* or it would be the worse for him.

When he left the office the young man was approached by several women who tearfully told him they thought he was going to be taken to a punishment camp and would not come back. Such things were common in wartime Germany. Many of those sent away were never seen again.

When he returned to his department Van Grieken was sent for by the manager who expressed sorrow at what had happened and told him he would be transferred to another department in a few days. In the meantime he was to take care to behave himself and cause no more trouble.

A day or two after these events took place Van Grieken was transferred to another department where he was put to work clearing scrap metal from a press used to stamp out metal parts. Helena came to see him several times and each time she brought a small parcel containing some food, a piece of cake, a bread roll with meat filling, a bar of chocolate. On one occasion she gave him five Marks to buy something with as she had nothing else. The last time he was to see her, she came to the hotel to tell him she was being transferred to another place and brought with her a parcel, about the size of a shoe box. It was full of food. Then she left. The young Dutchman often wondered if she had been transferred because the authorities thought she was getting too friendly with a foreign conscript worker.

When young Gilbert returned to his room and showed his companions what he had been given they asked him where the girl was. He told them she had gone home. "You fool," they cried. "You should have brought her in, we would have gone out and you could have had the room to yourselves." The embarrassed young man, who hadn't the slightest idea of what he might be expected or supposed to do if left alone in a room with a girl, tried to make light of the affair. He had to endure several days of teasing from his room mates about his innocence before they finally gave up and turned their minds to other things.

Some days after the fighting incident two police officers arrived at the factory with instructions to take Van Grieken to the police station for questioning. As before, one policeman marched in front and the other behind our miscreant. On the way out of the factory some women tried to stop the policemen and asked them where they were taking their prisoner. The policemen brushed the women aside, told them this was official duty and they had better mind their own business.

At the police station the young man was interrogated for three hours by a small, ugly policeman with a very harsh voice. He was closely questioned about the incident which had led to the German's complaint and also about his parents and grandparents, even to the details of the maiden names of his two grandmothers. After repeating such details as he could remember over and over again he was suddenly told to clear off and not come back again. If he ever came back, he was told, it would be much the worse for him. A long time later he found out the German police had scoured his family records to find out if there was any Jewish blood in him. Had there been any it is highly probable that the story of Gilbert Van Grieken would have stopped right there.

About this time the Dutchman became friendly with a young German youth of similar age. The German took him home to visit his parents who were friendly towards the foreigner and invited him to stay for meals on several occasions. After one such visit, walking home in the blackout, he walked straight into a tree, skinning his nose. He wondered at the time if it was a punishment handed down by the Almighty for having skinned the nose of the German!

Among the places the two friends visited was a local cinema where the German youth had a part-time job. The manager offered Van Grieken a similar part-time job, to fill in his off duty hours, but he refused as he didn't like the idea of having to walk home at night, on his own, in a strange city which was blacked out.

Despite the proud boasts of Reichsmarshal Hermann Goering that the skies over Germany would be inviolate, the Royal Air Force would come over, always at night and when the air raid sirens sounded everybody was ordered to take shelter. The raids were very small compared with the thousand bomber raids which were to come later in the war but retirement to the shelters, even during a small raid, gave some of the more worldly wise young men the opportunity to get friendly with German girls and to comfort them during the raids, or so they said that was what they were doing!

The friendship between the German and Dutch young men was abruptly terminated by the German. One day the two met on the street but the German walked straight past his friend without a word or a nod. When asked why he did this the German said, "I've heard you have been fighting with an *Arbeitskumerad* so I can't mix with you." With that he was gone.

In March 1941 the Japanese Foreign Minister, Mr. Matsuoka, paid a visit to Berlin where he was given a State reception. Such was the importance the Germans placed on this visit that arrangements were made for the employees of many factories, including AEG, to have time off to witness an appearance of the visitor, together with the Führer Adolf Hitler, on the balcony of the Reich Chancellery. There was a vast mass of people present, as ordered by the authorities, so it was impossible for Van Grieken to get very close but he did see the Japanese Minister, and Adolf Hitler, even if only from a distance.

After saving enough money from their wages to buy train tickets to Amsterdam, Van Grieken and one of his fellow Dutch colleagues decided to try to go home. They knew the train would stop at the Dutch border and had planned to get off the train there and walk across into Holland, where they hoped they would find help to get them to their homes. They packed all the food they could lay hands on in parcels, enough to last them several days, enough to last them until they could make contacts in Holland, and boarded the train.

Unfortunately the train arrived at the border sooner than they anticipated and was immediately boarded by the German police asking for permits to leave Germany. The two absconders who had no permits tried to hide, Van Grieken in the toilet, but the Germans were wise to that trick and they were soon flushed out. The two were placed under guard at the station where they were made to turn out their pockets to see if they had enough money to pay for the return journey to Berlin. Fortunately for them they had, with only a few coppers to spare, but in the excitement they had left their parcels on the train and all their food was gone.

Soon the pair were on their way back to Berlin, this time under guard, and were delivered by their guard to the factory gates where they were checked in. The gate guard grinned at them and said, "You must like it here," before leading the runaways to the same manager's office where the interrogation over the fighting incident had taken place. The manager asked why they had been so foolish and after listening to their poor explanations, told them if they tried anything so stupid again they would be in serious trouble. He then sent them back to work and the pair promised themselves they would do it properly next time, hoping they had learned something from the experience.

In May 1941, his six months period of service being done, Van Grieken applied for leave saying he needed to go home to get some new clothes as everything was wearing out. This was refused. His behaviour, he was told, had not been of the best and, what was worse, he had been guilty of fighting a German *Arbeitskamerad*. He thought this unreasonable, particularly as his friend who had been on the abortive attempt to return home with him was allowed leave, so he kept going back again and again with his plea to be allowed leave to obtain some new clothes. Eventually, after about a month, the German manager relented and gave him a permit but before he was allowed to go he was made to sign a form promising to return when his period of leave expired.

Returning home, this time with the necessary permit and having no trouble with the border police, our reluctant conscript worker took the opportunity of telling his story to the Dutch Labour office in Amsterdam. He was, he told them, damned in the eyes of the managers in the AEG factory because of the minor affair with the German *Arbeitskamerad* and could they find him work somewhere else where this stain on his character wouldn't be held against him.

The Labour Office were sympathetic, they had probably had other similar cases to deal with and, by this time, the sympathies of the Dutch people were firmly on the side of the Allies, a shift in opinion possibly helped by the fact that the Royal Air Force were dropping on Holland not bombs but parcels of food donated by the people of the Dutch East Indies anxious to help the inhabitants of their homeland in their period of trouble. Whatever the reason, the Labour Office arranged for the young man to be transferred to a new job. The Germans were not unduly concerned where he worked so long as they were getting the benefit of his labour so they were quite agreeable to the transfer, particularly as their need for workers in the occupied countries was, by now, becoming acute.

When his period of leave was up Van Grieken found himself once again at Amsterdam Central station but this time his train travelled west and his destination was to be the French port of La Rochelle with its massive installations designed to protect the pride of the German navy – the U-boat fleet.

Chapter 3

GILBERT GOES WEST

Little did he know it but the apparently friendly staff of the Amsterdam Labour Office were doing Van Grieken no favours when they arranged his transfer from Berlin to La Rochelle.

While in Germany he was, within certain limits, a free agent. He was free to do as he liked outside his working hours, free of restrictions on his movements, so long as he didn't try to leave Germany without a permit, and generally subjected to very lenient treatment, even when he transgressed the rules.

Life in occupied France was a very different kettle of fish as he was to find out when he, and the party of workers he travelled with, arrived at their destination.

Conscript forced labour in the occupied countries was placed under the control of the, to become infamous, Organisation Todt. This branch of the German military machine was a none combatant engineering corps whose main task was the construction of the vast defensive structures designed to make the continent of Europe invulnerable against attack by the Allies.

Mustered on military lines the Organisation Todt,, or O.T. as it was called colloquially, became notorious for the brutal treatment handed out by the German officers and NCO's of the corps to the workers under their command. The vast majority of the labour force working under their direction were slave labourers taken from Russia, Algeria, Morocco, the Balkan countries and also people from the occupied countries who had refused to do the bidding of their German masters.

These slave labourers were regarded by the Germans as prisoners under punishment and treated accordingly. They were given only the barest of necessaries in the shape of clothing, the minimum of food rations and housed under the most appalling conditions. The Germans regarded them as subhuman, to be treated as harshly as possible and worked until they dropped. They were given no dignity. They were regarded as expendable.

Such was the environment in which the young Van Grieken found himself. Although the conscript labour force were treated far less harshly than the slave workers and allowed a certain degree of freedom, the impact of such sights on the mind of an 18 year old youth is not difficult to imagine.

When the party from Amsterdam arrived at their destination they were taken to a former French army barracks at Rochefort, some 20 miles from La Rochelle, and this was to be home to the young Dutchman for the next six months. It didn't, however, take long for him to get into trouble with the O.T. authorities by switching on a light after the curfew hour in a room which had not been blacked out. This incident earned him one night in the cells but he was released the next morning.

At 6 o'clock every morning the workers were taken by bus from Rochefort to La Rochelle where they were put to work on the construction of the huge protective pens being built in a number of French Atlantic ports to house German U-boats during their periods of maintenance and rearming between patrols.

Van Grieken family visit U-boat pens at La Rochelle

Several thousand men were to be employed over a period of some four years in the construction of these massive structures, similar to those built at Brest, Lorient and St. Nazaire. Each pen, there were usually 12 at each port, was 350 yards long, 170 yards wide and had a height of 20 yards. The roof was 12 feet thick. Every pen could accommodate two ocean going U-boats, providing total protection for 24 boats at any one time.

The Royal Air Force, and later the United States Air Force, made several raids on these installations but did little damage to the pens themselves owing to the extreme strength of the structures. It was not until 1945, when the Royal Air Force was armed with the 22,000 lb deep penetration bomb developed by Barnes Wallis, of dam busting fame, that a weapon was found which could penetrate the roof of the immensely strong pens constructed by the O.T. men.

Most of the Allied air effort was directed against the installations at Brest and Lorient since these were closer to England and, consequently, a greater weight of bombs could be carried by the raiding aircraft. Some raids were carried out against the other ports, mainly aimed at damaging power supplies, workshop installations, etc. to reduce the capacity of the harbours to turn round shipping, including the U-boats. On one such raid on La Rochelle the only damage seen by the conscript forced labourers was when one bomb scored a direct hit on their latrine lines at the building site. This incident caused several cases of instant diarrhoea and the Allied conduct of the war lacked appreciation from the victims!

The workers slaved day after day mixing and pouring the vast quantities of concrete used in the construction. The work was dull and monotonous so that an environment was soon created where petty bickering was resorted to in an attempt to break the monotony. One day the conscript labour force, who considered they should be better treated than the slave labourers, staged a demonstration outside the O.T. offices demanding more food. The O.T. guards responded to this demonstration by firing shots over the heads of the protesters, who were shouting for more food or no work. This response rapidly put an end to the demonstration but the point must have been taken as the food provided to the workers was improved.

There were some lighter moments, however, during Van Grieken's stay at La Rochelle. It wasn't all pouring concrete for 12 hours a day. On one occasion the O.T. driver taking the workers back to Rochefort was clearly fairly drunk. He drove his bus at a speed of about 50 miles an hour while singing at the top of his voice and waving one arm about as though he were conducting his own singing. The passengers were greatly relieved, and not a little surprised, to get back to the barracks in one piece after this hair-raising journey.

The scene at the construction site reminded the young man of pictures he had seen in children's history books of the building of the pyramids. There seemed to be thousands of men crawling about like ants, or perhaps a colony of bees, all over the huge concrete structure which was to form the submarine pens. Materials, such as reinforcing steel bars, bags of cement, siftings, wooden shuttering and supplies of water to mix the concrete had to be hauled up a huge ramp made of tree trunks. The first time Van Grieken went up the ramp he was terrified as the whole structure shook and rattled as though it was about to fall down. It was still there six months later when he left so he concluded the engineers who had built it knew what they were doing.

In the summer of 1941, when Hitler decided to turn his attention to the conquest of Russia, the younger and more fit of the O.T. guards were drafted into the Wermacht, the combatant German army. One such young man, about 22 years of age, who had been one of the armed guards overseeing the O.T. labour force on the submarine pens and who had never shown any aggressive demeanour towards the unfortunates under his care, approached Van Grieken and told him, in a whisper, he had been drafted to a combat unit of the army. He pressed on the young Dutchman a packet saying, "This is for you." After the German had gone, Van Grieken examined the gift and found it contained a full package of 50 grammes of tobacco. Why the German had selected the Dutchman to bestow his gift on was a mystery which might possibly be explained by the fact that the two had a certain similarity in appearance.

Massive structures of the U-boat pens.

Not all the German guards were so tolerant or well disposed towards the conscript workers. One day a group of them were skylarking about in the communal wash house when a guard came in. The guard took the names of several of the men and, as a consequence, their pass to leave the barracks was withdrawn for one month.

For a time Van Grieken and his group were taken off the job of pouring concrete into the roof of the pens and transferred to a warehouse in the civil dock area, where they were put to work unloading and stacking bags of cement. As the security at the warehouse was much less oppressive than at the military construction site the workers were able to slip away from work on occasion and visit the local shops in the Ville au Bois district of La Pallice, the docks area of La Rochelle. Here they found the French people sympathetic to them and were able to buy some items of food to supplement the diet offered by the O.T. canteen. They also managed to become friendly with a French girl called Marie, whose parents ran a bar, and she gave them free drinks in the bar. These expeditions, although few and far between, gave the men some contact with friendly people, who were suffering as much as themselves at the hands of the mutually hated Germans, and did something to raise their morale.

The late summer and autumn of 1941 was a period of nervous stress among the Germans in France, especially those responsible for guarding the military installations on the Atlantic coast. Firstly there had been a substantial increase in the number of merchant ships sailing from the Gironde, mainly destined for Japan with war materials urgently needed by the Japanese, who were intercepted by the Allied navies and secondly there had been a number of unexplained sinkings of U-boats. Under normal circumstances U-boats enroute to, or returning from, the convoy routes were considered to be fairly safe as nearly all the Allied defensive naval forces were concentrated on escort duty around convoys. However U-boats, known to be well away from their patrol areas, were being sunk in circumstances the Germans couldn't understand.

Suspicion fell everywhere and not least on the foreign conscript workers who had the opportunity to pass on the French information regarding anything they had seen at the docks. It may have been because of this possibility the Germans decided to remove the workers to a less sensitive area.

In fact, the interception of the merchant shipping was the result of the efforts of a very efficient French Resistance Group based on Bordeaux who were supplying London with accurate information about shipping movements and precise details of the cargoes the ships were carrying. The unexplained sinkings of the U-boats was due to the development of airborne radar which could detect a U-boat, surfaced at night to recharge its batteries, long before the U-boat crew knew there was an aircraft in the vicinity. The searching aircraft could attack the submarine, at its most vulnerable time, before it could dive in self-protection.

The German decision to move the conscript workers was put into effect without warning. One day, in mid-November, an O.T. NCO read out a list of names, including Van Grieken's, and told the men to report at 6 a.m. for transport elsewhere. No details were given. Once more packed into a crowded train the workers were left to speculate on their likely destination. They had heard on the German news bulletins of the German attack on Russia and fervently hoped they were not going to be sent there, particularly with the winter coming on.

The fears of the conscripts were in no way allayed by the fact that at every station the train stopped at armed guards, German army soldiers, were posted to ensure no passenger left the train. They could do little but wait and see what was in store for them but fortunately their waiting was not for long. At around 3 a.m. the next morning the train pulled into St. Malo and they were told to get off. One again the men were piled into lorries, to be taken to a former French barracks, renamed by the Germans as "Bayerwald Kazerne," at St. Servan just to the south of the walled town of St. Malo.

On arrival at the barracks the workers were issued with a palliasse* and told to fill it with straw. This was their bedding for the three weeks they were to stay there. In charge of their guards was a Waffen SS officer who had been badly wounded on the Russian front. From the way he walked it was evident his legs had been badly shattered and his face was disfigured by burns to the extent he could hardly speak. The officer was of a disagreeable nature who appeared to regard each of the conscript workers as being responsible for his misfortunes.

Each day groups of workers were taken into St. Malo where they were put to work preparing hotels and other buildings for the reception of units of the German forces shortly due to arrive. When they returned to the barracks in the evening they would be lined up to receive a ration of soup and be counted to make sure they were all there. On one occasion one of the O.T. guards wasn't satisfied with the way the men were lined up so he started belabouring them with a broom handle. They soon lined up in a manner deemed satisfactory by the guard. On another day the guards found 20 men missing, the absentees having taken the opportunity of escaping into the night when the attention of the guards was diverted elsewhere. Where they had gone nobody knew.

The O.T. guards lost no opportunity to harass the conscript workers who they probably regarded as potential troublemakers and likely informers to the French of anything they had seen connected with German military matters. The matter of the 20 absconders did not help to improve relations between the guards and the workers who, although not so closely guarded as the slave workers or prisoners of war, were nevertheless watched by armed guards wherever they went. One evening an O.T. guard saw Van Grieken spill some water on the wash house

* By definition a palliasse is already filled with straw or it is not one. Hence, the workers should be given sacks to fill with straw to make or form palliasses.

floor and started kicking him. The young man fled up a concrete staircase with the O.T. man in hot pursuit. Fortunately for the Dutchman he was fleeter of foot than the German, who was encumbered by steel studded jackboots which slipped on the concrete steps. Van Grieken managed to escape into one of the barrack rooms while the German searched for him but, as there were about 100 men in each room, the German was unable to identify his quarry who escaped, this time, unscathed.

Day of arrival in Guernsey — 6 December, 1941 (l to r) J. Van Velsen, G. Van Grieken, J. Brand

Again, without warning, one evening an O.T. guard read out a list of names and told the men to parade in the yard, at 5 a.m., with all their possessions, for transport to another location. As before no details of their destination was given.

At 5.30 in the morning the Germans were ready to move off. This time they were taking no chances of anybody escaping. The conscript workers were marched off, with armed guards posted at 10 yard intervals on both sides of the column, and taken to St. Malo harbour where they were loaded into the hold of a small coastal freighter. The ship had an identification number H8 and that was all the unwilling passengers knew about it. Where they were going they had no idea and, once again, speculation was the main topic of conversation as the men waited to find out what their masters had in store for them.

Finally the ship left St. Malo and docked again at about 3 o'clock in the afternoon. The hatches were opened and some of the men were taken out of the hold. Food was passed down to the remainder, who were told to stay where they were. Word got around that the ship was at a place called Jersey and would sail the following morning for another island. In the meantime the conscript workers left in the hold had to make themselves as comfortable as possible until they reached their destination.

Finally the ship sailed again and, in the middle of the following afternoon, docked in another harbour. The huddled group of workers in the hold were brought up and landed on the quay where they were surprised to find men working alongside the ship speaking English. One of the group of workers asked the men if they were prisoners of war. "No," one of the dock workers replied. "We are Guernseymen. We live here. This is Guernsey and we are occupied by the Germans."

Thus the young Van Grieken arrived in Guernsey. He vaguely remembered having heard on the German news about some British Islands the Germans had invaded but wasn't quite sure where they were. All he, and his fellow conscript workers, hoped was they were not going to find themselves in the battle line, being shot at by both the British and the Germans.

Chapter 4
ISLAND FORTRESS

Not being in the confidence of the German authorities, Gilbert Van Grieken could not know the reason he and his fellow conscript workers had been sent to Guernsey was to help put into effect a secret order, signed by Hitler on 20 October 1941, that the Channel Islands were to be turned into an impregnable fortress.

The Dutchman arrived on 6 December 1941. He remembered the date with particular poignancy as it was the Feast of St. Nicholas a day on which, in happier times, the children of Holland would be looking forward to receiving presents with great excitement. There were few children to be seen in this island on that day in 1941 as most had been sent away to the safety of England a year and a half before.

The Germans had come to Guernsey, the first of the Channel Islands to be occupied, on 30 June 1940. At the height of their triumphant conquest of northwest Europe they arrived convinced their armed forces were about to invade and conquer the one remaining European enemy not yet subjugated, Great Britain. The arrival of the German forces in the islands, carrying with them maps of England and some believing they had landed on the Isle of Wight, was to be the first step towards that goal. In the event it turned out also to be the last.

For the first eight months of the war, from September 1939 to May 1940, the conflict had very little effect on the people of the islands. Rationing of some foods and petrol had been introduced, as in England, but otherwise it was largely a case of business as usual. In Guernsey the island authorities, headed by the nearly 70 year old bailiff, Victor Carey, were convinced the only threat to their homeland came from the remote possibility of sporadic air raids. When war was declared they went through the motions of putting the community on a war footing by imposing blackout regulations, some trenches were dug to provide makeshift air-raid shelters, gatherings where numbers of people might congregate together, such as sports meetings, were banned and the cinemas closed.

When nothing happened in the first few months of the war the people clamoured for the restrictions to be lifted. Normal life was largely resumed to the extent that shopkeepers in St. Peter Port agitated for the blackout regulations to be varied to allow them to light their windows "so that normal trade conditions could be restored." So great was the confidence of the population of the islands that the war would not affect them, that the Guernsey Chamber of Commerce went so far as to suggest the island be advertised as being a place of safety to which people living in potentially dangerous areas of England might wish to consider moving. Heads were no wiser in Jersey where the Tourist Board, in March 1940, were placing advertisements in the British press extolling the virtues of the island as being "the ideal resort for wartime holidays this summer."

This complacency was rudely shattered when the Germans started their operations against the Low Countries and France in May 1940. The widespread use of parachute troops, and the rapidity of the advance of the German armies, threw the island authorities into panic. No contingency plans had been drawn up to cover the situation of the islands being threatened and nobody knew what action, if any, the British Government would take if they were called on to defend them.

As May passed and June came, with the news of further advances across France by the German armies, the panic developed into hysteria. Efforts by the island authorities to find out what Britain intended to do were met with bland assurances from officials at the Home Office, the department of government responsible for relations between the British Government and the islands, that the situation was under control. Elements of the British Expeditionary Force still in France would be moved to the islands, anti-aircraft protection would be provided, almost any story was told to allay the fears of the islanders while Britain frantically sought a solution of the question of what to do about these, hitherto unconsidered, territories now threatened by the enemy.

As time went by thinking in London gradually polarised to the idea that the islands should be evacuated. Even if the Germans stopped their advance at Cherbourg, as it was widely believed at the time they would, the presence of a powerful enemy air force only 40 miles away would render it impossible, except at great cost in shipping and lives, to either defend the islands or keep them provisioned.

To Britain, the islands had little value. Although British possessions they were not part of the United Kingdom and had only come under the rule of England by an accident of history. As part of the Duchy of Normandy when William, 7th Duke of Normandy, invaded England in 1066 to claim the Crown as his right, they were included in the territories in France owing allegiance to the Crown of England. When, in 1204, King John lost his continental possessions in Normandy he offered the islanders a constitution whereby, in return for the continuance of their loyalty to him, they could govern themselves according to their own customs and laws. It is probable that the King saw the islands as a useful forward springboard from which to mount an offensive to recover his lost lands in Normandy, if the opportunity came. It never did come but successive sovereigns, down the ages, reaffirmed this status so that from that day to this the islanders have enjoyed full internal self-government. They have their own legislatures, laws, legal systems and taxation.

While the islands had been of strategic value to Britain in the days of sailing ships, particularly during the period of the wars with France when the then barren and uninhabited island of Alderney was turned into a naval base to provide the Fleet with a safe anchorage on the south side of the English Channel, this was no longer the case in a war dominated by air power. They were now more of an embarrassment than an asset. Their loss would be of little consequence militarily and would not generate very much in the way of adverse propaganda. it is probable that, in the summer of 1940, fewer than five per cent of the population of Britain had ever heard of the Channel Islands or knew, or cared, where and what they were. The British, facing a threatened invasion of their own land, had bigger problems to worry about than the fate of a few thousand people living on some islands which, to all intents and purposes, were almost foreign territory.

However, since they were British and Britain was responsible for their defence, some sort of gesture had to be made and the preferred solution, one which called for the minimum of military participation by already hard pressed armed forces, favoured evacuation. At the time Britain was well versed in the skills necessary to conduct a successful evacuation. More than a million women and children had been evacuated from the main towns and cities to safe areas in the country at the start of the war. Here they would be safe from the bombing of towns by the German air force that had been expected. By the summer of 1940, when the bombing had not materialised, many of those evacuated had returned to their homes. There was plenty of accommodation available in the evacuation areas. More recently the Royal Navy, with the help of an armada of merchant and privately owned vessels, had evacuated 350,000 British and Allied soldiers from the beaches at Dunkirk and so saved them from capture by the German army. Evacuation was the order of the day and the expertise and shipping necessary to perform the task were readily to hand.

So the decision was taken to demilitarise the islands by withdrawing what small military presence was there and to offer evacuation to safe areas to any islander who wished to take advantage of the offer. It is, perhaps, unfortunate that when these decisions were notified to the island authorities they did not, at once, inform the population at large. It has been claimed, in their defence, that they were placed under an oath of secrecy. If this were true, to have accepted such a restriction was an act of supreme folly and demonstrated an appallingly low standard of leadership.

The first sight which alerted the man in the street to the fact that something was afoot was that of convoys of military vehicles, loaded with munitions and other military stores being embarked on ships bound for England. This action created the rumour that the troops were being withdrawn and the civilian population was to be left to its fate. Having read stories, and seen pictures, of the treatment of civilian refugees on the continent the people of the islands developed an atmosphere of unreasoning fear as to their future. The first sign of panic was a run on banks so great as to force the authorities to issue orders limiting the amount of £25 that any person could draw. This was followed by unprecedented hoarding of any commodity, not limited by rationing, that might be thought to become in short supply.

When the authorities in Guernsey finally decided to tell the people what decisions had been made they did so without giving any advice or guidance as to what people should do. It was left to each individual to make up his own mind. The people were told of the arrangements made for the evacuation of school children and that mothers with children under school age could accompany their children in the evacuation. Otherwise people had the choice of leaving or staying behind to face a future which promised they knew not what. The way in which the announcements were made was described by one contemporary writer as giving the suggestion of "a sinking ship in which women and children take precedence over men."

It was fortunate in Guernsey that the Education Council had on its staff civil servants with far more presence of mind than had been demonstrated by the island's politicians. As soon as the idea of a mass evacuation of children was considered they quietly went about the business of organising lists of children and teachers who might be transported to England. When the decision was announced the work done by these people ensured that the evacuation of the school children was achieved with remarkably little difficulty. Parents were told the children must assemble at their schools, the first batch at 4 a.m., with one suitcase, their gas masks and ration books. A contemporary account tells of the silence of the night being broken by the sound of tiny feet, accompanied by excited chatter, as the first of the children went to their schools to be taken to England, a land few of them had ever visited. The main problem facing those responsible for organising the evacuation was the indecision of many parents. The evacuation was voluntary and some of the parents changed their minds again and again, according to whether the last person they spoke to was in favour or against the idea of evacuation. To be fair to the parents it must be remembered they were being asked to choose between sending their children to an unknown destination, for an indefinite period, in the charge of comparative strangers or to keep them at home and stand the risk of unspecified dangers which might, or might not, materialise. It is to the credit of the vast majority of parents that they chose the safety of their children over all other considerations. In all some 5,000 children, around 80%, were safely evacuated.

While all these activities were going on in the islands the German High Command in Berlin gave orders, on 20 June 1940, to the Naval Flag Officer commanding northern France, that the capture of the British Channel Islands was to be achieved without delay. This was to prove eventually to be a decision which would cost the Germans dearly in terms of manpower and materials and bring them no tactical or strategic advantage whatsoever. In fact quite the reverse, it was a decision which was to provide the Allied armies with almost an open door when they came to invade the continent of Europe four years later.

Fortunately for the islanders the Germans took their time in implementing these orders and the evacuation of all those who wished to leave went on without further hindrance. By 26 June some 22,000 people had left Guernsey and 9,000 from Jersey. Alderney was totally evacuated. The first German presence was felt in Guernsey on 28 June when six German fighter-bombers appeared over the island. By unfortunate coincidence the Guernsey States had arranged for the regular mail steamer visiting the island on that day to transport a cargo of tomatoes to the mainland so a large number of lorries and horse drawn vehicles were assembled at the harbour waiting to load the produce. The German pilots, seeing this assembly of vehicles, wrongly assumed it to be a military convoy and attacked with bombs and machine gun fire. The attack was devastating, 34 people were killed or fatally wounded and another 33 injured. The attacking German pilots insisted they had attacked a column of heavy vehicles but their claim to innocence was somewhat sullied by the fact they also attacked, while at sea, the St Peter Port lifeboat, hardly an unrecognisable vessel, killing one of the crew.

The occupation started on 30 June when a single German aircraft landed at Guernsey airport. The head of the island police, Inspector Sculpher, was despatched to the airport with a letter addressed to "The Commanding Officer, German Forces, Guernsey." The letter stated the island had no armed forces whatsoever. By the time the Inspector reached the airport, however, the German pilot, who had found the airport buildings deserted, had taken off again, presumably to report his findings to his base.

Some five hours later four German transport aircraft landed at the airport and the Inspector was sent off again with his letter. This time he was more successful and delivered the missive to Kapitan Liebe-Pieteritz, the German officer sent to receive the surrender of Guernsey.

The occupation started peacefully enough with Inspector Sculpher taking a party of Germans, in a police car and a requisitioned taxi, to the Royal Hotel. There the invaders were joined by the Bailiff, Victor Carey, and the man who was destined to become Guernsey's tower of strength during the occupation, the Procureur de la Roi – HM Attorney-General – Major Ambrose Sherwill MC. Reading between the lines after a lapse of nearly half a century it would appear the States of

Guernsey, which at that time consisted almost entirely of elderly men well past the prime of life, decided they were not well fitted to handle the problems which would arise with the island under military occupation. To provide a civil administration they decided to appoint a Controlling Committee with Ambrose Sherwill as President. The elderly Bailiff, who had also been appointed Lieutenant Governor, with responsibilities for civil matters only, was nudged gently sideways and Major Sherwill became the effective, if not titular, head of the island administration.

The Germans, who were clearly well prepared, issued a long and complicated list of instructions to be notified to the population. These included the imposition of a curfew between the hours of 11 p.m. and 6 a.m., prohibition of the sale of spirits and petrol and the embargo on the movement of boats of any description. The Germans also informed the island administrators that the entire cost of the occupation must be paid by the island. German currency in the form of Occupation Reichmarks, given a wholly fictitious value of RM7 = £1, was introduced allowing the German troops the opportunity of going on an unprecedented shopping spree, an opportunity they took with considerable enthusiasm much to the annoyance of local shopkeepers who knew they could not replace their stocks.

The first months of the occupation went by peacefully enough. The population had been told by the Bailiff and the President of the Controlling Committee not to offer any resistance to the occupying power and warned that the "continuance of the privileges granted to the civilian population depended on our good behaviour."

At first the Germans allowed the population to retain their radio sets but in September 1940 they were ordered to surrender them as a penalty for giving assistance to a somewhat pointless Commando reconnaissance into the island in July. This had been carried out by three Guernseymen who were landed from a submarine with the task of finding out the strength of the occupying forces. The sets were returned to the owners in December. They were finally to be requisitioned again by the Germans in June 1942, this time on the grounds of "military necessity" although exactly what the necessity was remains a mystery.

The occupation, and the terms imposed by the German invaders, created some severe problems for the civil authorities. The first, and greatest, needing immediate attention was the financial aspect. The island had relied for its income on exports of produce, mainly tomatoes, to the United Kingdom and paid for the import of foodstuffs, fuel, clothing, etc. from the proceeds of those exports. Not only were the exports now lost, together with their revenues, but the States were faced with the added burden, imposed by the Germans, of having to pay the wages of all the civilian employees, cooks, messengers, clerks, interpreters, labourers, engaged to support the German army, from public funds. Rigorous economies had to be imposed, the salaries of civil servants were drastically reduced and a sales tax imposed on everything except rationed food and clothing.

The supply of food became a serious problem as normally the greater part of the island's requirements had been imported. There were some bright spots, however. In 1939 the States had urged farmers to grow larger than usual food crops with the result that in 1940 the areas under potatoes and corn were substantially higher than usual. In addition Jersey, which normally relied to a large degree on exports of potatoes to the United Kingdom, was able to export considerable quantities to Guernsey. The stock of potatoes in the island in 1940 became almost embarrassingly large. The same situation prevailed with regard to tomatoes. When the occupation started some 2,000 tons of fruit were left in the island's glasshouses, either ripe or ripening, enough to give, while the season lasted three pounds each day to every man, woman and child remaining in the island. Great efforts were made by the Controlling Committee to find ways of preserving tomatoes so that some stocks would be available during the winter months but these met with little success since the preserving of this fruit requires either salt or fuel, both of which were in short supply.

As autumn moved on into winter a number of events occurred which caused the Germans to modify their hitherto fairly benevolent attitude towards the islanders and the civil authority.

On 9 August a single RAF aircraft made an attack on the airfield damaging one troop carrying aircraft and setting a hangar and petrol dump on fire. The Guernsey fire brigade took their time in reaching the airfield to attack the fire and when they did arrive the sight of a number of German aircraft returning to the airfield, aircraft which might in the minds of the firemen be British intent on doing more damage, caused the firemen to leave their appliances in the hands of the German soldiers to fight the fires as best they could. Despite the ruling of the Germans that visiting the airfield was forbidden a large number of islanders went there the next day on sightseeing expeditions with the result the President of the Controlling Committee was forced to publish a letter in the local press advising people to keep away from the area. A week later the German Commandant published a statement which claimed that, contrary to a BBC broadcast which had stated the airport had been extensively damaged, little damage had been done. One German soldier had been killed and one wounded. Much later it was discovered that 27 Germans had been killed and 17 wounded in the raid.

At the beginning of September a party of eight men escaped from Guernsey in a 20ft fishing boat and successfully made a landfall in England. The propaganda value of this escape was exploited to the full by the British who dropped leaflets, and copies of the London newspapers describing the event, on the island. The leaflets also carried a message from King George VI expressing the sympathy of himself and Queen

Elizabeth for the trials the islanders were enduring and looking forward to their speedy liberation.

The German authorities tried furiously to recover the leaflets and newspapers. They issued a proclamation stating it was an offence to communicate the contents of, or hand on, such propaganda to others. A penalty of 15 years imprisonment for transgression of this proclamation was announced. Apart from the obvious boost to morale this escape created in the minds of the islanders, the only noticeable effect was the imposition of more severe restrictions on the movement of fishing boats which were now concentrated in the harbour of St Peter Port, where a close watch could be kept on them.

About the same time the Germans got wind of the presence on the island of two British soldiers and started an island wide search for them. The two were, in fact, Guernseymen who had been landed from a motor torpedo boat which was supposed to come back three days later to pick them up but had failed to do so. The Germans had been alerted to their presence because the third member of the party had stumbled into an anti-aircraft post and had been captured by the gun crew.

The reaction of the Germans to this incursion was, to say the least, strangely muted. It must be remembered, however, that the German garrison on Guernsey at the time numbered less than 1,000 men, who had a civilian population of 23,000 to police. It was probably, therefore, in their own interests to play the matter down as much as possible. At the same time the civil authority was equally anxious that the event, which was unlikely to bring any great benefit to the island population, should not cause disruption in the tolerably harmonious relations they had developed with the Occupying Forces.

The outcome was a very courteous exchange of correspondence between the German Commandant, Major Dr Albrecht Lanz, and the President of the Controlling Committee, Major Ambrose Sherwill. The men had much in common, both had military experience and both were lawyers. This similarity of outlook may well account for the tone of the letters exchanged between the two on the subject, a tone which, after the war had ended, Ambrose Sherwill admitted to being "a bit smarmy."

The result of these letters was an official notice being issued by the German Commandant to the effect that it was known to the German authorities that members of the British armed forces were hiding in the island but providing they reported to the Island police force within a specified limit of time they would be treated as prisoners of war. If they didn't surrender they would be regarded as agents of an enemy power and dealt with accordingly. This notice was backed up by a letter from the Bailiff, published in the island newspapers alongside the Commandant's notice, calling on all islanders to observe and comply with the notice. In all eight men surrendered themselves, six who had been on the island since the start of the occupation and Lieutenants Nicolle and Symes, the two men the Germans were looking for.

It would seem this was the point at which the German High Command began to look afresh at their policy towards the Channel Islands. They were clearly not particularly happy at the way the German Commandant in Guernsey was playing his hand and ordered the arrest of 12 islanders, related to or closely connected with Lieutenants Nicolle and Symes and also Ambrose Sherwill. These persons were transported to France and imprisoned in the Cherche Midi prison in Paris.

The German authorities held a military Court of Inquiry into the whole affair and finally decided, somewhat surprisingly, to honour the agreements made between the Commandant and Ambrose Sherwill. Those arrested were released from prison and returned to the island, the two soldiers sent to a POW camp but Ambrose Sherwill was relieved of his post as President of the Controlling Committee as "further co-operation with the German authorities was no longer possible." The islanders were warned, in the announcement of the findings of the Court of Inquiry, that any future illegal behaviour would result in immediate countermeasures.

All the time the RAF maintained an interest in Guernsey. Several raids, mostly of the "tip and run" variety were made in the last three months of 1940. The airfield was a favourite target. After one raid nine lorry loads of aircraft wreckage were seen being transported to France while on another occasion a just completed hangar, camouflaged to make it look like a glasshouse, was destroyed only hours before it was due to be formally inspected by the Commandant.

While all these events were, in the context of the total war effort of both sides, minor incidents they will have been duly recorded in the war diary of the *Feldkommandantur* and thus brought to the attention of the *Abwehr* the German military intelligence service and, in time, to the notice of the Führer himself.

By the middle of 1941, with his troops and air force committed to the Russian campaign and thoughts of an invasion of Britain shelved, Hitler became concerned with the possibilities of a British attack on the European mainland. He knew full well that a major invasion was out of the question at that time but was, nevertheless, concerned that Britain might attempt a small scale operation and considered the most likely place for such an attack would be the Channel Islands. As part of his defensive measures against an invasion of the continent by Allied forces, at some time in the future, the Führer instituted his *Festung Europa* –Fortress Europe – policy and directed that the Channel Islands were to be converted into *"eine unangreifbare Festung"* – an impregnable fortress. The work was to be given the highest priority and was to start immediately. Monthly reports of the progress made were to be made to the Führer personally.

Responsibility for implementing the Führer's instructions was given to the Organisation Todt who immediately started to scour Europe for labour. Among the many thousands of men who were to be swept into the net was the young, bemused Van Grieken who, knowing nothing of these decisions, found himself standing on the windswept quayside at St Peter Port, on a chill December day, waiting for the next order from his German masters.

Chapter 5

HARD LABOUR

The decision of the Führer to fortify the Channel Islands brought not only Van Grieken and his group to the archipelago but, in all, some 18,000 of his fellow Organisation Todt workers, two divisions, some 30,000 men, of German infantry, plus supporting troops and elements of the German Navy.

So far as the German military were concerned garrison duty in the islands was far preferable to life, or death, on the Russian Front. They regarded the islands as being what the British soldier would refer to as a "cushy billet" and were anxious to be seen enthusiastically obeying the Führer's orders. To the O.T. workers it was just another place where they would fare no better or worse than elsewhere.

The islands had been fortified many times in the course of the

Conscript forced labourers in Bosq Lane (l to r) 2 Flemish workers, G. Van Grieken, J. Versluis

previous 700 years. As each new threat from France had manifested itself so new forts, towers and strongpoints had been constructed to meet the needs of the age. All these were redundant to the military requirements of the 1940's and this was the situation the German military engineers had come to correct.

The extent of the fortifications that were eventually to be constructed was immense and accounted for nearly 10% of all the resources in materials and firepower allotted to the entire Atlantic Wall. Despite the protestations of several very senior German army officers, including Field Marshal Rommel, that the Channel Islands had no strategic or tactical value to either Germany or the Allies, Hitler insisted that his fortress concept should be effected. His plan for post-war Europe included absorbing the islands into Germany with the object of creating on them a western version of Heligoland, a fortified and secure base for the German navy.

One of Rommel's main concerns, when he was appointed German Commander in Chief France, was the weakness of the coastal defences in the region of Arromanches. Many of the planned batteries and strongpoints in this area had not been constructed as the manpower and materials needed to build them had been diverted to the islands. His protests went unheeded as the German High Command, and Hitler, were convinced the Allies could not attack in strength at that point on the coastline of Europe because of the lack of harbours capable of handling the vast amount of material needed to support a major invasion. Thus the area was furnished with defences only on a scale suitable to repulse a minor diversionary attack. The Germans were not to know the Allies would pick that very region for their landing or that they would bring their harbours with them. Adolf Hitler, with his fixation about the Channel Islands, had left the invading Allied armies an almost open door.

But back to the young Van Grieken standing in the chill winter air on the quay in St. Peter Port wondering what was coming next. Soon some lorries arrived and the conscript labourers were loaded aboard. Their destination was L'Ancresse, where they were to be accommodated in requisitioned houses and bungalows. The accommodation provided was spartan to the extreme, providing little in the way of comfort. Each room, according to size, was furnished with up to six wooden double tier bunk beds with wood slats as a base. The only bedding provided was a straw filled palliasse and two army blankets. No chairs, tables, carpets or other furniture were provided.

Each morning the labourers were taken by lorry to Pleinmont where, high on the cliffs, they were put to work preparing a site for the construction of a coastal battery. Below them, as they toiled, the men could see the now darkened Hanois lighthouse which, for nearly 80 years, had flashed out its warning to passing ships of the treacherous rocks on the west coast of Guernsey. Built in 1862, the lighthouse had been the subject of nearly eight years of, sometimes acrimonious, correspondence between the Royal Court (forerunner of the States) and the British Government. The first point at issue was the extent of the authority of Trinity House, who wanted to have a lighthouse erected on the Hanois rock, in Guernsey. When this had been finally sorted out, after about four years, the next issue was who was going to pay for the light. This took another four years to settle before the lighthouse was built.

The group Van Grieken was put to work with consisted of about 50 men, some conscript forced labourers and some slave labourers. The slave workers, Moroccans, Algerians and Greeks who had been living in occupied France were rounded up by the Germans and, together with petty criminals found in French prisons, drafted into the Organisation Todt for construction work. Their condition was pitiful. Clothed in little more than rags, underfed and denied any proper sanitary facilities, they were accommodated in what was, to all intents and purposes, miniature prison units and given the minimum of subsistance rations. The conditions under which the slave workers were housed were so bad that a German doctor, after an outbreak of typhus in one of the camps, warned the German authorities of the danger to their own troops if the sanitary conditions of the slave workers camps was not improved.

The work the men were given to do was backbreaking. Only hand tools, pickaxes and shovels, were provided for the men to prepare the site located on a granite outcrop. Each swing of the pickaxe might loosen half a shovel load of granite, if that, so the progress of the work was slow. If the O.T. guards thought the slave workers, in particular, were not working fast enough they were more than ready to urge them to greater efforts with the aid of the pickaxe handle or a whip.

The Germans had laid down a light mineral railway at the site and the spoil from the workings had to be loaded into rail trucks and taken to the cliff edge where it was tipped

Each midday the conscript workers were lined up and given a ration of thin watery soup fit only for drinking, there was nothing in it to spoon up. This 'meal' had to be taken while working. There was no lunch break. The slave workers were also given soup which they had to drink out of any receptacle they could find, old food tins, a disused saucepan, anything which would hold liquid. The O.T. slaves were usually so ravenous they would battle to reach the food lorry but it has been said that the old hands held back and waited as they knew the soup at the bottom of the container was thicker. The O.T. guards went off elsewhere for their food, which was undoubtedly more substantial and sustaining than that given to the workers.

At the end of each day the slave workers would be taken back to their camps, given their usual meagre ration and left to sleep on the floor of whatever building they were billeted in. The conscript workers fared better, although not a lot. Van Grieken and his group were taken back to their billets and lined up in a kitchen which had been set up in the garage of the bungalow in which they lived. There they were given a ration of warm food, vegetable, lentil or macaroni soup or, sometimes, boiled potatoes and vegetables with a tiny piece of meat. At the same time they were given a half pound of bread with some butter and jam and, occasionally, a piece of meat. This was to be their breakfast for the next morning. They would take the warm food back to their rooms to eat. After that they were free to do as they liked but since there was little of attraction to be found at L'Ancresse, particularly in wintertime, and the strenuous nature of the day's work they had done most of the workers simply went to bed, to prepare themselves for another day of picking and shovelling at the battery site.

The people of Guernsey, or any other of the islands for that matter, knew nothing of Hitler's fortress directive. What little evidence of it to come before their eyes was the arrival of more and more troops and foreign workers together with the unloading of vast quantities of cement, steel reinforcing bars and other building materials. During the closing months of 1941 and the first half of 1942 manpower, armaments and materials poured into the islands.

Much effort was made by the Germans to keep the slave workers out of the sight of the civilian population. Apart from their unkempt appearance and nondescript clothing, even to the extent that some were reduced to wearing bits of old motor tyre as shoes, the harsh and brutal treatment handed out to them, especially those who tried to escape or committed minor misdemeanours, was not a good advertisement for German justice and frequently acclaimed respect for law and order. One house in the Vale parish was turned into a punishment centre where transgressors were subjected to treatment of such savage brutality that few, if any, ever risked a return visit. One of the more favourite punishments meted out by the O.T. guards was to hang the offender upside down by his ankles and then flog him unmercifully. It is not surprising these activities were kept well away from the islanders for the mentality of these guards, who were drawn from the dregs of German society, was limited to the concept of utter brutality towards their charges. They had no other capability; no doubt that is why they were so employed.

The inhabitants of Guernsey were soon to see the results of the work done by the conscript and slave labourers. Massive concrete structures, all well guarded by German soldiers, appeared around the island. The most impressive of these was the 'Mirus' battery at Frie Baton, St. Saviour's. This battery mounted four guns, unfortunately destroyed after the war. The guns were of 16 inch calibre and capable of firing a shell weighing over one ton to a range of some 25 miles. This was considered enough to outgun any Allied capital ship which might seek to reduce the island's defence works by bombardment. The guns themselves had an interesting history. Manufactured before the First World

War, they were mounted on a Russian battleship. At the end of that war the ship had fallen into German hands and was scrapped during the interwar years. As is the custom when warships are scrapped, the costly guns, which rarely have been used to anything approaching the limit of their useful life, are removed and stored for future use usually in another ship. These guns remained in store until brought out to be mounted on this major battery in the island's defences; defences against an attack that was never to come.

The installation of large numbers of heavy artillery pieces in the islands, together with anti-aircraft batteries to defend them, created a requirement for the importation and storage of substantial quantities of ammunition and propellant charges. Explosives regulations, observed as closely by the Germans as anyone else on the grounds of safety, require that such materials must be stored with a considerable distance between dumps, if stored above ground. The alternative is underground storage in protected bunkers.

Since the area of ground space required by the regulations would have been difficult to find on a small island like Guernsey, the Germans opted for the alternative and put Organisation Todt labourers to work digging a network of tunnels throughout the island. One tunnel was excavated under St. Saviour's Church, probably because the Germans considered it unlikely the Allies would attack a church. Another runs between Havelet and Fort George. The latter were also to be used as underground fuel storage for the replenishment of U-boats, probably as part of the German postwar plan to turn St. Peter Port into a major U-boat base. The construction of the tunnels not only met the explosives regulations but provided protection for the stores against air attack.

In addition to the ammunition stores another major excavation work was undertaken to provide a 600 bed underground hospital in Guernsey. Although very well equipped and fitted out with complex ventilation systems the hospital was used only for a very short period in 1944. It was found that, due to either the lack of daylight or the high humidity that prevailed in the underground wards, despite the ventilation system, wounds would not heal and even patients admitted with relatively minor ailments looked and felt worse after discharge. A similar installation in Jersey was found to suffer the same problems.

All this work was performed by the ever increasing numbers of slave labourers brought into the island in response to the Führer's directive, a directive nobody but the highest ranking officers dared question. The cost of the construction programme was phenomenal and the islands civil authorities drew the attention of the Germans to the fact that the fortifications, and other construction works, were not essential for the defence of the islands but were part of the Atlantic Wall. They argued it was unreasonable that they should be made to pay for far more than their fair share of the cost of the overall *Festung Europa* project. The Germans, surprisingly, accepted this argument and arranged for a proportion of the occupation costs to be returned as credits in Paris where they could be used to buy food, and other goods, for the civilian population.

During the first months of 1942 the rapid expansion of the Organisation Todt labour force in Guernsey, together with the need to provide labour to unload the increasing cargoes of building materials and other stores from ships arriving at St. Peter Port, gave Van Grieken the opportunity to get away from the oppresive regime of the O.T. guards. Being a small, slightly built man he did not have the ideal physique for the heavy manual labour required to prepare the gun battery sites so he, and four of his fellow workers, were transferred to work on shipping in the harbour and placed under the day-to-day control of the German army. A new, and far less rigorous, period of his work for the self-proclaimed master race was to begin.

Gilbert Van Grieken in Bosq Lane – late 1942

Chapter 6

ST. PETER PORT – 1942

Transfer to the control of the German army quartermaster's department in St. Peter Port not only brought the Dutchman relief from the worst excesses of the Organisation Todt guards but also provided some, albeit small, measure of improvement in the living and working conditions of himself and the four other conscript workers who were transferred at the same time.

Gilbert Van Grieken with French and Polish Workers on rooftop in Berthelot Street

The accommodation they were moved to, at first in Berthelot Street, was furnished in the same spartan fashion as that at L'Ancresse but the hours of work were less, 8 a.m. to 6 p.m. with one and a half hours off for lunch. The rations provided were a vast improvement on those from the O.T. kitchens. This was particularly so while the workers remained in Berthelot Street as they had to collect their food from a house in

Lefebvre Street. Billeted in this house were a number of German soldiers, presumably from the Catering Corps, who were working at the slaughterhouse on the Castle Emplacement. As is common among soldiers the world over, particularly those of an Army of Occupation, they made sure their own cookhouse was well supplied. Again the diet was mainly soup or stews but now with substantially more meat content, thanks to the acquisitive habits of the military occupants of the house.

After about six weeks the conscripts were moved again, this time to a house in Bosq lane, and were given their meals at Belle Greve House, near the Red Lion. Here they were fed the same food, except for the bread ration, as the German soldiers who were fed there. There was no fraternisation between the German troops and the conscript workers, each kept to their own set of tables at mealtimes and had no social contact outside the mess hall.

By 1942 the people of Guernsey had come to terms with the occupation and had, by and large, accepted the situation. Their main immediate problem was food, clothing and fuel. All were in desperately short supply and people went to extraordinary lengths to find, and steal if necessary, a few bits of wood to provide a small fire. One of the more scandalous events of the time was the arrest by the German *Feldpolizei* – Military Police – of 18 members of the Guernsey police force who were charged with stealing foodstuffs from a German store and firewood from a dump opposite the Police Station. During the course of their investigations the *Feldpolizei* discovered that 10 of the policemen in their custody had also been stealing food from the island's Essential Commodity Committee's stores together with food and wines and spirits from individual shops.

The 18 policemen were tried by a German court on the charges relating to theft of German property, one was acquitted and the remainder sentenced to varying terms of imprisonment. The Germans then handed over to the civil authority the evidence they had accumulated relating to the thefts from civilian stores and shops. Ten of the policemen were tried by the Royal Court on these charges. Again, one was acquitted but the remainder found guilty and sentenced to further terms of imprisonment. The German trial had been meticulously fair and the Royal Court trial conducted in the proper manner with the accused defended by Ambrose Sherwill. In passing it may be mentioned that in 1955 the nine found guilty by the Royal Court appealed to the Judicial Committee of the Privy Council, the highest Court of Appeal for the inhabitants of the British territories outside the United Kingdom, to have their convictions set aside. The Judicial Committee gave long and careful consideration to the evidence, and the claims of the convicted policemen that their actions were intended to sabotage the German war effort, before coming to the conclusion that, except for the conviction in respect of one charge which was quashed, the remaining convictions and sentences should stand. The opinion of the Judicial Committee may have been swayed by the disclosure that the pilfering from island stocks had been started before the occupation and thus could have hardly been inspired by a desire to do damage to the enemy.

The policemen were, perhaps, unfortunate to be made examples of since the stealing of food was endemic in the island. Growing crops were at greatest risk, particularly from the German troops who were allowed to be out-of-doors during the hours of curfew. Instances were recorded of O.T. slave labourers, poorly guarded by negligent O.T. guards, escaping from their quarters to go rummaging in dustbins and raiding gardens for produce. On occasion the island police were forced to complain to the German authorities that the O.T. guards were deliberately releasing their prisoners at night so that they could go on stealing forays to supplement their meagre rations. Their task was made easier by the fact that the owners of gardens or glasshouses were prevented by the curfew regulations from mounting guard over their property at night.

The conscript labourers employed by the quartermaster were not above a little thieving when the opportunity presented itself. Each morning they reported to the Bouillion Stores, near the Longstore, to be assigned their day's work. This might be at the harbour, helping in the unloading of ships, or in one of the many stores scattered around the island. As with any unloading activities in a harbour, or transfer to a storehouse, breakages and spillages would occur and anything easily concealed rapidly disappeared into the pockets of the conscript labourers. Whenever the opportunity arose the conscript labourers would pass on to any slave labourers they came across some of the illicit food they had managed to get hold of. Once, when passing down the Grange in a lorry with German guards in the front, Van Grieken threw a packet of honey to some Moroccan slave workers and watched a fight take place among the slaves to retrieve it. The guards did not see the action.

Since any shortages will have been noted by the German clerks recording deliveries, blame for them would lay at the door of the German army guards responsible for supervising the unloading of ships and transfer of goods to store. They, in turn, took their displeasure out on the labourers. Van Grieken observed one such incident when one Unter Officer Schreiber asked a Moroccan labourer where he had been the previous day. The man replied that he had been sick. "I saw you on the front. You weren't sick then," said Schreiber and stamped his jackboot heavily on the unfortunate Moroccan's left foot before telling him to clear off and go to work at the harbour. About an hour later the man's foot was so badly swollen he had to remove his rubber boot and ask for permission to return to his barracks. This was permitted but the incident indicates the sort of treatment meted out to the labourers by the army guards.

Gilbert Van Grieken's next move was to L'Ecole Intermedaire —

Filles (later known as the Girls Grammar School and now the home of the States Vehicle Registration and Licencing Department) in Rosaire Avenue. A group of 15 conscript forced labourers, 5 French, 5 Belgians and 5 Dutch were billeted in a house opposite the school, where they had to report each day for work detail. They were also fed in the school assembly hall and, once again, enjoyed German army rations. Now and again they would be given second helpings of such rare luxuries, for those items, of potatoes and meat balls which they were allowed to take back to their rooms for later consumption. Another occasional luxury was a ration of tea or coffee. The tea was always very sweet, but not the coffee. One Christmas the tea was even laced with rum, presumably to celebrate the festive season. Also in the school was a small canteen where, about once a month, the forced labourers were allowed to buy small quantities of tobacco and cigarette papers.

Shortly after being transferred to Rosaire Avenue, Van Grieken had another encounter with Unter Officer Schreiber. The German, clearly suffering from a hangover as he was a heavy drinker, saw the Dutchman in front of the school and demanded to know why Van Grieken had not said "Good Morning" to him. The Dutchman said he had not seen the German who immediately became abusive, calling Van Grieken a variety of uncomplimentary names and asked where he worked. On being told it was Summerfield House in Mount Durand (a German Officers' Mess) the German yelled "Clear off you pig," and aimed a kick at the young man's backside. Once again Van Grieken's fleetness of foot saved him from injury but, nevertheless, he felt the German's boot scraping his trousers.

Detailed for work in the Officers' Mess, on some days, gave the Dutchman the opportunity for some choice pickings. The German army officers were usually quite relaxed in their own quarters and used to joke with the young man. Once they told him, with mock solemnity, that he should greet them each morning with "Heil Hitler." "No," he replied "I say every morning Heil Wilhelmina!" To that response one of the German officers grabbed him in a playful mood, and in the scuffle which followed Van Grieken fell and scraped the skin off the knuckles of one hand, which began to bleed. At the sight of this injury the Germans decided to leave him alone.

Red letter days were the mornings after the officers had had a party, usually with German army girls. There was always a mess to be cleared up with food, tobacco and cigarettes left lying about. The Dutchman took the opportunity of relieving the Germans of the burden of surplus food and tobacco. One day, while clearing up after a party, he found a holster with a pistol in it. At first he hid the gun in a hedge but later, thinking if he was blamed for the loss his fate would be worse than a few skinned knuckles, he handed it in. Some days later he was told the officer who the pistol belonged to didn't even know he had lost it. Nobody bothered to thank the young man for handing it in.

One Sunday evening, returning to his quarters in Rosaire Avenue, Van Grieken saw the commander of the unit based in the school standing in front of the house where the forced labourers were billeted, together with a group of soldiers. When the Dutchman reached the house one tall *Ober Feldwebel* — Sergeant Major — said, "That's him," grabbed the youth and made him stand in front of the commander. The German officer started to interrogate Van Grieken about stolen property found in his room and was clearly not prepared to accept the Dutchman's denial of any knowledge of stolen property. The commander made a sign to the *Ober Feldwebel* who started to punch the Dutch youth.

"Now will you tell the truth?" asked the German officer.

"Yes," answered Van Grieken. "I have a few potatoes in a cupboard."

"We are not looking for potatoes," said the commander then, bringing his hand from behind his back, disclosed a bundle of leather boot soles. "Andrew told us he got these from you. What is your explanation?"

Andrew was a Flemish lad living in the same room as Van Grieken and at that moment came walking down the stairs. When Van Grieken saw him he said in a loud voice, "What is going on, Andrew? They say you got these boot soles from me. You know I've never had any."

This was said in Dutch and the *Ober Feldwebel* turned to the officer and said I understand what he has said as I live only three kilometres from the Dutch border and know the language. Andrew, in the meanwhile, stood on the steps crying.

The commander obviously felt he had had enough of the affair for the day and told the NCO to let the conscripts go and they would sort it out in the morning. After making more enquiries the next day the commander ordered a fine of 50 Marks to be levied on those found with illicit property. Van Grieken was then ordered to the commander's office. The German officer made a joke of the affair and said he was sorry the Dutchman had been given a hiding but he was getting off lightly, without the fine imposed on the others, despite the potatoes, which he could keep.

In 1942 the Germans could afford to be lenient with such minor transgressors as they were at the peak of their successes in the war. In the west the U-boat offensive against Allied shipping was sinking ships at the alarming rate of 600,000 tons a month, well beyond the replacement capabilities of the shipyards. In Russia, the German armies had advanced deep into Soviet territory, certainly at great cost in casualties, and had suffered no major reverses. In North Africa, General Rommel's Afrika Korps was poised to capture Egypt and the Suez Canal. Over Germany the might of the Royal Air Force Bomber Command offensive against the major towns had yet to be demonstrated. In the Far East Germany's ally, Japan, was systematically invading the colonial territories of Britain and Holland. To the Germans the might of their armed forces must have looked unstoppable.

To be sure there were some factors which gave concern to the Germans. The United States had been drawn into the war by the Japanese attack on the US naval base at Pearl Harbour in December 1941 and Britain remained unconquered. It was probably the latter situation that caused the Germans to put into effect, in September 1942, the second part of Hitler's directive of 20 October 1941 which ordered that all British subjects not island born were to be deported. Exactly what purpose was supposed to be served by the transfer of these people from what was, in effect, one German prison camp to another has never been explained.

Earlier in the year, in June, the Germans once again confiscated all wireless sets in private possession. They justified this move on the grounds of "military necessity" and cited the Geneva Convention as their authority. They conveniently overlooked the fact that the section of the Geneva Convention which authorises the confiscation of radio equipment in occupied territories specifically refers to transmission apparatus, not receiving sets. Again, there was no obvious advantage to be gained by this order except that the islanders could not listen to news bulletins broadcast by the BBC, bulletins which were considerably at variance with the heavily censored news the Germans permitted the island's newspapers to publish. One amusing outcome of the confiscation of wireless sets was that a large number of enterprising islanders manufactured crude crystal sets to listen to the BBC. One shortage, however, was earphones and this was overcome by removing the handsets from island telephone boxes and using the earpiece to complete the set. So great was the loss of handsets that after the liberation the Telephone Council had to make an appeal for their return.

All this activity on the part of the islanders had little effect on the fortunes of young Van Grieken who managed to keep on relatively peaceful terms with his German masters. The officer who had ordered his beating over the boot soles affair saw him in the Queen's Road one day and stopped his car, an Austin 7 requisitioned from some inhabitant and now painted in German black and brown camouflage. He told the Dutchman to jump in and he would give him a lift. The German joked about the incident of the soles and said a few clouts were better than a 50 Mark fine. As for Van Grieken, he just hoped nobody would see him riding about in a car with a German officer as his contemporaries would not have treated him kindly if they thought he was becoming a favourite of, or a toady to, the enemy.

Around the middle of 1942, presumably as a reward for his tolerably satisfactory and obedient service, Gilbert Van Grieken was permitted two weeks home leave. Armed with the necessary travel permit he boarded, in St Peter Port, the same ship which had brought him to Guernsey. This time he wasn't made to travel in the hold but allowed to use the limited passenger accommodation in the company of German soldiers and some civilian passengers. One of these, a Belgian woman travelling in the company of a German soldier, spent most of the voyage to St. Malo hanging over the rail being violently seasick.

When the vessel arrived in St. Malo the conscript labourers were instructed to report to the Organisation Todt kitchens where, to their astonishment, they were given a parcel of food to take home. This extraordinary generosity they couldn't understand but in the Europe of 1942 nobody rejected an offer of food. Having collected their food parcels they went to the railway station to catch the train to Paris.

Railway journeys in wartime France were, to say the least, an adventure. The conscript labourers, travelling on an O.T. permit, went third class, being careful to avoid any compartments marked *Nur fur Wehrmachtsangehorige* – Reserved for Wehrmacht – and hoping they did not attract the attention of the all too frequent German Military Police forever on the lookout for unauthorised travellers. By this time the Germans were becoming very concerned at the expanding activities of the French Resistance movement and were constantly watching for any traveller with papers which had the slightest hint of irregularity about them. Every document was carefully scrutinised and the bearers of any about which there was the slightest doubt were taken into custody for investigation.

On reaching Paris another pleasant surprise awaited the travellers. German Red Cross girls, dressed in white uniforms with a large red cross emblazoned on the front, were handing out soup. The soup was intended for soldiers but, on being assured that the conscripts had military travel permits, the girls gave each of them a ration of soup.

On again to Amsterdam Central station where Van Grieken was stopped by two German soldiers on guard duty and told to open his case so they could see what he was carrying. At first he refused, saying he was a peaceful citizen travelling home and they had no right to stop him. This line of argument didn't impress the soldiers at all. They grabbed his case and, since it had no lock, opened it. When the soldiers saw the food parcel they immediately accused the Dutchman of smuggling and operating on the Black Market. After much protestation and showing his travel permit, together with an explanation of where the food parcel had come from, he was eventually allowed to go on his way. He left the station as fast as his legs could carry him.

At the end of his permitted two weeks holiday Van Grieken took a train to The Hague for the purpose of visiting the O.T. offices to seek an extension of his leave as he was sick. On the way he ran into a police check when it was spotted his travel permit had expired the previous day. After the young man explained he was on his way to the O.T. offices to obtain an extension of leave he was allowed to proceed, after all his particulars had been noted down. He was told to report to the police office with his extension and, if all was in order, there would be no further trouble.

At the O.T. office the Dutchman was given a two week extension without too much trouble. He was owed the extra time anyway as his contract of employment with the Germans allowed him two weeks holiday every six months and he had none for the past year. With the extension he was also given a warning not to try to travel again with an out-of-date permit.

The extension expired, the young Dutchman reluctantly set off to return to Guernsey and his labours with the German quartermaster. His journey, via Paris and St Malo, went without a hitch and he was soon back in Rosaire Avenue, hoping he could keep out of trouble until his next leave.

Chapter 7
TURN OF THE TIDE

While the Germans may have had reason for self-satisfaction with the progress of the war in 1942, by the spring of 1943 ominous signs for them were appearing on the horizon.

On the Eastern Front the Russians had taken advantage of the terrible winter weather, to which they were used and equipped for, to inflict heavy casualties on the German armies while driving them several hundred miles back from their front lines which had reached the outskirts of Moscow and Stalingrad. The German Sixth Army, under the command of General Paulus, comprising 18 divisions of German and Roumanian troops, had been forced to surrender at Stalingrad.

In North Africa, General Montgomery's Eighth Army had driven Rommel's Africa Korps out of Libya and had joined up with General Eisenhower's American First Army, which had landed in Morocco during the previous November to join the Free French forces in the French African colonies. The way was open for the ground battle to be taken into Europe.

In the Atlantic, the introduction of more sophisticated radar equipment in RAF Coastal Command aircraft was resulting in increased detection and sinking of U-boats with the consequent marked reduction in the amount of Allied shipping being lost by sinking.

While some of these activities could be kept from the knowledge of the greater part of the German people, the growing power of the Allied air forces could not. Cologne had experienced, in October 1942, the first of the one thousand bomber raids to be mounted by the RAF. The introduction into service of heavy four engined bombers, each capable of delivering 12 tons of bombs, caused terrible destruction in German towns and cities.

By January 1943 Winston Churchill and Franklin Roosevelt were so confident of eventual Allied victory that they announced, at a meeting in Casablanca, their war aim was "unconditional surrender" by both Germany and Japan. It was an aim since considered by many eminent authorities as being a tragic mistake. It embittered the war and rendered a fight to the finish inevitable. It permitted no negotiation between the combatants and, as far as the inhabitants of the Channel Islands were concerned ensured the occupation would remain in force long after any hope of victory had left the minds of the German commanders in the islands. They could not negotiate, only surrender. Their military code would not permit capitulation unless overwhelming enemy power were to force such action on them. Safe inside their fortress no such power confronted them, so they stayed to the very end.

G. Van Grieken with a friend in the Pollet — 1943

As the occupation went on the conditions under which the inhabitants lived gradually deteriorated. The basic shortages of fuel and food remained and to these, as the occupation dragged on, was added a marked shortage of clothing. Although ample clothing had been available in the early years, by 1943 stocks of new clothing, and almost everything useable as garments, were exhausted. Even secondhand items in wearable condition were hard to find. The situation became so bad that the German authorities prohibited their troops and conscript workers from buying goods on the civilian market but, nevertheless, some Germans tried to get round the prohibition by getting sympathetic islanders, of which there were some as in all occupied territories, to buy goods for them.

German troops and forced labourers — Harbour 1943
(standing) Unteroffizier Wagner, Obergefreiter Otto, unknown, unknown, Soldat Swartz
(front) G. Van Grieken, R. Wessels, W. Cloosterman, J. Brand, J. Versluis

All the while, the building of defence works went on. Gun positions, tunnels and air-raid shelters were constructed around the islands. There was one bonus from this activity which was of general benefit to both the civil population and the occupying troops alike. In the construction of the defence works, which used vast quantities of reinforced concrete, a considerable amount of timber was used as shuttering to form the moulds for the concrete to be poured into. Once the concrete was set the timber shuttering was removed and generally discarded to provide a valuable source of firewood which was scavenged by the civilian population whenever the opportunity presented itself for them to help themselves when the Germans were not looking.

Gilbert Van Grieken and his fellow conscript labourers continued their work for the German quartermaster, sometimes in the stores and at others transferring goods from the harbour to store. Whenever they could they picked up any odd packages or tins of food spilling from broken crates or split sacks. Sometimes this bounty was loose food like sugar which they put in their pockets where it mixed with dust and other debris. This didn't bother them in the least, the sugar and anything else they found was eagerly consumed, irrespective of contamination, testifying to the indestructable nature of the digestive systems of the young.

One quite amusing incident while Van Grieken was working in Mount Durand. Two senior quartermasters, together with some junior ranks, came out of the house one day and set up a makeshift rifle range. Using a small bore sporting rifle they took turns shooting at the target. The young Dutchman watched with interest as nobody seemed to be hitting the target, a strange performance for soldiers he thought. Eventually one of the quartermasters, Ober Zhal Meister Schnee, said to him in German, "Have you ever fired a gun?" "No," replied Van Grieken. "I have never fired a gun in my life. I've never been in the army. Guns I know nothing about."

"Right," said Ober Zhal Meister Schnee. "You try this thing and see if you can do better than us." Taking the rifle, the young man lay down in the prone position, as he had seen the Germans doing, took a long time to aim, then fired. One of the soldiers went to the target and called out, "Bull's eye." Without a further word the Ober Zhal Meister took the rifle from the Dutchman and all the Germans walked away. The Dutchman stayed where he was until they had all gone, fearful of some retribution being taken for his having made a fool of them. Fortunately for him the Germans had had enough for the day.

The conscript labourers, being free to do more or less as they liked after the day's work was finished, did have opportunities to mix with the Guernsey people. Dances were held in the old St Barnabas chapel at Clifton also at Sunnycroft in the Grange. At one of these dances a competition was held to forecast the date of the end of the war. Van Grieken guessed 8 May 1945 and, after the war had finished, collected the first prize of five pounds, paid in English money. On another occasion at a dance he walked into a door, which had previously always been open, and knocked the skin off his nose. He began to wonder if the fates were going to punish him eternally for having knocked the skin off the nose of the *Arbeitskamerad* in Berlin three years before!

Much to his surprise, in April 1943, Van Grieken was again given home leave. Once more he boarded the ship H8 in St Peter Port and set sail for St. Malo. This time, however, the Germans were well aware of the growing Allied air and sea power and formed the ships into a convoy which sailed at night. More vessels joined the convoy at Jersey and the assembled ships, each flying a barrage balloon to deter air attack, and escort vessels set course for St. Malo. It was a wild night with very rough seas causing the ships to pitch and roll with alarming frequency. At one point H8 was in imminent danger of ramming one of the escort vessels. Sirens were sounded, bells rung and the engines stopped just in time to avoid a collision between the two ships.

Eventually the convoy reached St. Malo safely and the passengers disembarked. This time there was no food parcel from the O.T. kitchens so Van Grieken, and the five other conscript forced labourers travelling with him, took the first available train to Paris. Once again the German Red Cross girls were handing out soup, this time without question. Another train onward to Amsterdam, the journey this time being broken at St. Quentin when a German Military Police ticket check resulted in six Dutch civilians being thrown off the train after being told they had no right to travel on a troop train. They had to wait six hours before another train, which they were allowed to board, came to take them on the rest of their journey.

The Holland the forced labourers returned to in 1943 was very different to the one they had left in 1940, or indeed to the one Van Grieken had visited in 1942. The mood of the people had changed from the shock of 1940 and the sullen resentment of the German occupation of their land which had developed by 1942, to one of determined resistance to German plans by the middle of 1943. In the early part of that year the Nazis had expressed the belief that the Dutch were a 'Germanic' race and should not be treated as a conquered people but rather regarded as likely candidates to accept the principles of National Socialism. The Dutch, however, were not prepared to offer any accord to this point of view.

Reich-Commissioner Seyss-Inquart encouraged the Dutch Nazi Party to form a Dutch Nazi State Political Secretariat with powers to issue decrees covering civil matters. Eighteen members were appointed to this secretariat, of whom three were assassinated before June, but the efforts of this organisation were thwarted by the Netherlands Government in London who broadcast appeals to their fellow countrymen to resist any orders issued by the traitors.

On March 17 a decree was issued closing down all trade and industrial undertakings not directly essential to the German war effort and all men thus released were required to report for deportation to Germany as forced labourers.

The Dutch responded by going underground. By the end of May 70,000 people were in hiding and by the end of the year the figure had grown to some 300,000. Among those who went underground was Gilbert Van Grieken's brother, Jan, who had also been recruited as a conscript forced labourer. He had also been at La Rochelle but later was transferred to Berlin to work on a railway station. While there he endured an air raid in which his barracks had been burned down, the occupants escaping the inferno in their night clothes. Having had enough of air aids, when he was sent home to Holland he promptly went into hiding and remained underground for the remainder of the war. When the Germans surrendered he joined the reformed Dutch army wearing a blue boiler suit, as a temporary uniform, with black helmet. The men were armed with Sten guns and wore an armband with the letters NBS *Nederlandse binnen landse strijdkrachten* – Dutch Interior Forces.

At the end of his permitted leave period Gilbert Van Grieken travelled back to St. Malo, making sure this time his travel permit was not out of date. Reporting in at the Bayerwald Kaserne at St. Servan he ran into the SS officer, who was still wobbling about on his wounded legs although his voice had improved. A group of the men were standing about chatting when the officer called out "Ein, zwei, drei, vier, funf" and pointed to five men, including Van Grieken, in turn and ordered them to stand in front of him. Taking his pistol from its holster he held it against the forehead of each man. "Now," he said. "There is a transport of your *Arbeitskameraden* coming from Brest. Go down to the cellar and fill palliasses for them to sleep on. If any of you are idle or tries to escape this is what will happen." With that he placed the muzzle of his pistol against the first man's head. The meaning of the threat was only too obvious.

Leading the way, the SS officer showed the men the steps to the cellar where they found several dozen men hard at work stuffing palliasses with straw. After about an hour Van Grieken took a look at the top of the stairs and, finding nobody was watching, walked slowly back to his barrack room. If the German officer noticed his absence he must have decided not to put his threat into effect.

The next day the Dutchman heard from some Flemish men that everybody was being held for transport to Germany to work on some dams that had been bombed. On 17 May 1943 a force of specially converted Lancaster bombers of No. 617 Squadron RAF, under the command of Wing Commander Guy Gibson, had attacked three dams supplying water to industry, canals and hydroelectric generating stations in the Ruhr. The attack breached two dams, the Moehne and the Eder with the result that 335 million tons of water were released to swamp great areas of land, flooding railways, factories, power stations and inundate whole towns. The urgency of the need to repair the dams as soon as possible caused the Organisation Todt to scour the occupied countries for any spare labour which could be diverted to undertake the mammoth task of repairing the damage caused by the attack. Thus the labourers freed from Atlantic Wall projects, now advanced, were assembled at St. Malo for transport to Germany.

Van Grieken, who had teamed up with another Dutchman who was en route to Jersey, was not anxious to be included in the draft. He had enough of Germany on his first visit and didn't wish to repeat the experience. When the men were ordered to report to another camp, about half a mile away, they took the opportunity of taking their suitcases to an hotel in St. Malo. Their plan, if they were included in the draft for Germany, was to tell the authorities they would have to go to the hotel to collect their cases before being transported. If this were to happen they intended to make a run for it, as had so many others before them.

Somewhat to their surprise, and pleasure, when they presented themselves to the authorities at the new camp the Germans, after some discussion, allowed them to continue their journey. Although the forced labourers did not know it, Hitler's directive of 21 October 1941 was still in force and no German official would be so unwise as to direct labour away from the Führer's priority programme without prior agreement from those responsible for completing that task. All Van Grieken knew was his travel permit was endorsed "Permitted to return to Gustav." He was well content with that, particularly as the two thought their ruse with the suitcases had been successful.

The two labourers had to wait in St. Malo for two weeks before they could get a boat back to the islands. This they did not mind as it gave them an additional holiday, although St. Malo in 1943 would hardly have been the ideal recreational resort. One evening during their stay they met some O.T. guards in a canteen who asked if they were Polish. On being assured the two were Dutch, the O.T. men became more friendly and told of an incident they had recently witnessed at a camp for Russian P.O.W. outside Granville. In each room there were 20 men and when the guards went to count heads in one room they found only 19 there. All those present denied any knowledge of the whereabouts of the missing man, so a search was begun. Behind an old wooden hut in the compound the guards found some freshly dug earth so they made the Russians who shared the missing man's room excavate the area. This disclosed the remains of the missing man with parts of the body carved away. The German guards, without any further ceremony, shot the 19 Russians for the crime of cannibalism. That, in the view of the O.T. men telling the tale, showed what manner of people the Russians were.

Also, while waiting in St. Malo, Van Grieken met a French girl who offered to put him in touch with the French Resistance. They, she said, would provide him with a safe hiding place where he could escape the Germans. The young man, who did not see himself in the role of a hero, declined the offer, possibly deciding the devil he knew was better than the devil he didn't. In any case he was probably wise to refuse as there were many collaborators among the French population and he could easily have found himself betrayed as an enemy of the Reich, if the girl was not all she claimed to be.

Eventually, around the end of May, the Dutchman found himself back in his billet in Rosaire Avenue and reporting daily for work detail. One of the tasks given him was to load, unload and transfer goods from the harbour to store. Transport was sometimes provided by a lorry owned and driven by a Guernseyman, Fred Mahy. Mr. Mahy had cunningly fashioned a secret compartment in the floor of the lorry in which any loose oddments or packets of food could be concealed for later distribution. On one occasion they were driving down St. Julian's Avenue with a German guard named Schwartz in front with driver Mahy. The German had his rifle sticking out of the window, as it wouldn't fit in the cab. By accident the soldier pulled the trigger and a bullet went into the wall by the Boer War Memorial. The forced labourers nearly jumped off the lorry in fright but soldier Schwartz thought the whole affair a huge joke and laughed his head off. The passengers, who didn't like guns going off near them weren't so amused, they were just grateful they were still alive.

Working party — White Rock — 1943
(l to r) Fred Mahy, Unteroffizier Wagner, Obergefreiter Otto, R. Wessels, W. Cloosterman, J. Brand, Soldat Swartz (on lorry) J. Versluis, G. Van Grieken

One day the Dutchman was detailed to go to Summerfield House in Mount Durand and help dig an air-raid shelter. Among the working party were three men Van Grieken could not identify. He was somewhat surprised as it was unusual for the men to be accompanied by a guard. The men spoke to each other in whispers and kept a wary eye on the German guard overseeing them. After some time it dawned on the Dutchman that the three were speaking German and surreptitious enquiries revealed they were German soldiers under punishment for having taken photographs of the gun installations they were manning. This puzzled Van Grieken as he too had taken photographs, although not of military installations and nobody had stopped him.

While working on the air-raid shelter the Dutchman saw what he thought was an air raid on Fort George, possibly one of the 'dumping' raids carried out by the Allied air forces who had been instructed to use the islands as a last resort target of opportunity if they were unable to identify their primary target on the mainland of France. He saw a bomb drop but heard no explosion and saw no smoke. He always thought there had to be an unexploded bomb somewhere in Fort George and, indeed, this materialised many years later.

A strange incident occurred one day when a group of the conscript labourers were walking away from the White Rock back to their billets. As they walked up St. Julian's Avenue they were stopped by a tall, well dressed man who spoke to them in Dutch. He was obviously well educated and spoke with a cultured accent. He said he was staying at the Royal Hotel and had been watching the men through binoculars. He wondered why they were so excited. Had they stolen food in their pockets and was the excited behaviour to fool the enemy? He said his name was Mann, but the labourers hurried off without answering. A long time later they heard a rumour the man had been shot as a spy in the south of France but the rumour did not extend to explaining which side he had been on.

As the year 1943 advanced the Germans became more nervous. Not only were the Allied air forces visiting the islands more frequently, mainly for reconnaissance purposes to determine the state of the defences, but the German High Command knew an invasion was planned. What they did not know was where. The islands seemed a likely place for the Allies to try to recapture but the Germans were unaware of, certainly British, thinking of the advisability of retaking the territory. They had learned the cost of maintaining and supplying islands close to enemy held territory during the seige of Malta and had no intention of repeating that experience. Additionally aerial reconnaissance had shown the heavy defences any invasion force would encounter so the Allies made their decision very early on to leave the Channel Islands alone and to let the Germans sweat it out there.

In addition to avoiding another costly island operation it suited the Allied plans to have the Germans kept in a state of uncertainty. A massive deception operation was being mounted to conceal from the High Command where the main blow of the Allied invasion of Europe would fall. Already the body of a man, who had died of pneumonia but exhibited the clinical signs of death by drowning, dressed in the uniform of a officer in the Royal Marines, had been floated ashore from a submarine onto the coast of Spain. The body carried documents bearing the genuine signatures of high ranking Allied commanders, pointing to the south of France as being the main landing area. An actor, a General Montgomery look alike, was sent to Gibraltar so that agents sympathetic to the Nazi cause could report his presence in that theatre of war. An extensive network of phoney radio stations, most of them mobile, was set up in the south and east of England to create the impression in the minds of German intelligence the presence of an army corps being assembled to invade France in the region of Calais.

The deception was to continue up to and beyond, the day of invasion in June 1944. The aim was to stretch the German defences as thinly as possible and the tying down of two divisions of infantry, plus all their supporting services, in the Channel Islands suited the Allied commanders very well. The Germans were welcome to the islands for all the good they would do them.

Not all went the Allied way however. In November 1943 two German torpedo boats successfully attacked and sank a British cruiser, the HMS Charybdis, in the English Channel and the bodies of some of the sailors were washed ashore in the islands. The Germans, despite their bestiality towards such people as the Jews and those unfortunates who had fallen into their hands as slave labourers, had a code of honour towards war dead of fighting services, even those of their enemies. When 19 bodies of British sailors were recovered in Guernsey, the Germans ordered a funeral with full military honours and allowed the civilian inhabitants of the island to pay their respects to the dead. The response was overwhelming and over 700 wreaths were laid at the graves of the sailors. To this day, the anniversary of the sinking of the ship is marked by a memorial service, attended by members of the ship's company of a Royal Navy warship visiting the islands for this special purpose.

To Gilbert Van Grieken, and his fellow conscript workers, all these events made little difference. They worked at whatever tasks were set for them, their labours perhaps being made a little heavier by the fear of the Germans that they might have to prepare themselves for seige conditions and so provisioned the islands to withstand a long period without replenishment. In doing so they were only concerned with their own requirements. They gave no thought to the needs of the civilian population, they would have to fare as best they could. However, as 1943 came to a close, things were not yet desperate as both islanders and their unwilling guests, the forced labourers, made the best of their conditions while they worked to survive each day. They made what simple entertainment as they could to amuse themselves and longed for the day when they would be free of the domination of the German nation. By this time the tide of war was turning very much in favour of the Allies, and this was known to the subjugated peoples in the islands through illicit listening to the broadcasts of the BBC, but they were still to have to wait for some time before relief would come.

Chapter 8
THE GATHERING STORM

As the task of fortifying the Channel Islands reached completion and the threat arose of the islands having to withstand a seige while the Allied and German armies battled on the mainland of Europe, each side confident it would win, the need for contingency plans arose in the German minds. They had brought into the islands many thousands of slave workers to build the fortifications and now the work was nearly completed the question arose of what to do with these labourers.

On the European mainland most of the planned fortifications had been completed, at least as far as the available materials would permit, therefore there was no immediate requirement for additional labour there. Nevertheless the feeding, housing and guarding of these thousands of men, many desperate in the abysmal conditions under which they were forced to live, absorbed valuable resources which could be illspared by the Germans, now no longer able to command the entire resources

Unexplained structure near Les Vauxbelets

of Europe for their own use. Some means had to be found of relief from this burden and it looked, at one time, as though the accepted German solution to any such problem, extermination, was going to be put into effect – at least in Guernsey.

Gilbert Van Grieken visits Les Vauxbelets building.

The building of a mysterious, and as yet unexplained, structure was started near Les Vauxbelets close to the site of a slave labour compound. Fortunately for the occupants of the compound the building was never completed, for it had the hallmark of being intended as a crematorium. The signs are that it was the intention of the Germans to dispose of their surplus slave labour in Guernsey, and probably Alderney, by the employment of their already perfected system of gassing the victims with Cyclon B gas, followed by cremation of the remains.

Execution of this scheme was abruptly interrupted by an order from General Jodl, the German Chief of Staff, just after the start of the Allied invasion of Europe, that all slave workers were to be returned to the mainland of Europe. General Jodl was not acting on any humanitarian grounds but reflecting Hitler's instructions that, whatever happened, the Channel Islands were to be held to the last. The General was somewhat more realistic than some of his colleagues and had already formed an accurate judgment of Allied intentions. He was of the opinion the Allies would simply try to starve out the German garrisons in the islands and saw no sense in having several thousand extra mouths to feed from the limited amount of food available. Since the means of extermination were not yet ready, an exodus was the only quick solution. This also had the advantage of compliance with the Führer's directive that under no circumstances were the slave workers to fall into Allied hands. So it was ordered that substantial number of slave workers and penal prisoners were to be transported to concentration camps in Germany, to a fate that was only to become known when the Allied armies overran these camps and exposed to the world the full horrors of the Nazi regime.

The construction of the crematorium was halted, its purpose no longer existing. Van Grieken had met some Dutch forced labourers at the Imperial Hotel at Pleinmont who were part of the construction gang engaged on this project. They disappeared at the same time as the other slave and forced labourers, provided by the Organisation Todt for German construction companies, when they were withdrawn to mainland Europe. It was, perhaps, a stroke of fortune for Van Grieken that he had been transferred from German civilian work to German military duty and thus escaped being deported with the main body of O.T. workers in the summer of 1944.

In the months preceeding these events the Germans concentrated on consolidating their positions in readiness for the expected attack. For the first four months of 1944 the islands were virtually ignored by the Allies but towards the end of May things started to liven up. On 22 May four aircraft flew up the Little Russel and shot up Brehou Tower, where the Germans had mounted anti-aircraft guns, inflicting casualties among the gun crews. Gilbert Van Grieken watched one such raid when a bomber flew low over the sea towards Fermain. The aircraft was being subjected to intense anti-aircraft fire and he was told later by a German soldier, with malicious enthusiasm, that the aircraft had been shot down in the sea to the south of the island.

Gilbert Van Grieken re-visits the German Underground Hospital in St Andrew's.

Five days later a considerable force of bombers attacked Fort George with the aim of destroying the radar stations installed there. Very heavy damage was done to the Fort and heavy casualties suffered by the German troops stationed there. Some 80 Germans were killed and around 350 wounded. The more seriously wounded were transferred to the underground hospital, in St Andrews, where conditions prevented their wounds from healing, as described in Chapter 5. Van Grieken had to visit the hospital for treatment and saw the patients lying on steel frame beds, all looking sallow and sickly as no daylight reached them. He was not very impressed with what he saw, or for that matter with the German army medical services as a whole. He once had a tooth taken out at the army dental surgery located at the corner of the Grange and Queen's Road. It had been a painful experience. He much preferred the attention he had been given by a German navy doctor at a surgery close to the Guernsey Brewery. This doctor, treating him for a sprained ankle, had been gentle and patient with the Dutchman, who was sorry to hear later that the doctor, a *Kreigsmarine Leiutnant*, had been lost at sea in a U-boat which had been sunk.

The Allies kept up the attack on the radar installations at Fort George with daily raids until they were sure the station would be unable to provide early warning to the German defences of the air armada which was to fly over nearby Normandy a few days later, an armada which was to be clearly heard in the islands in the early morning of 6 June.

The immediate effect of the Allied invasion starting on 6 June was to put the island garrisons on full alert to resist the attack on the islands they thought was imminent. Gun positions were fully manned, all coastal areas patrolled by heavily armed troops and vital points like the telephone exchanges guarded by sentries. Movements by civilians were severely restricted as the Germans watched and waited for the Allies to strike.

Shortly after D-Day, Gilbert Van Grieken had a ringside seat for what was to be the most devastating air raid to be experienced in Guernsey. Standing at the corner of the Grange and Brock Road, he heard the sound of anti-aircraft guns firing and looked up to see three aircraft, quite high in the air, turning over to start a dive. The only place to shelter, not that it provided much protection, was a tree in the garden at the end of Brock Road. Sheltering under the tree, the Dutchman watched as the bombers came down and the anti-aircraft fire, especially from the area of the harbour, became more intense.

About half a minute after seeing the aircraft, Van Grieken saw the bombs drop and a few seconds later heard the explosions as the bombs detonated in what appeared to be the area of the White Rock. The raid did not, in fact, achieve its apparent objective since the primary target, a damaged U-boat which had been moored in the harbour a few days previously had been moved. The raiders did, however, sink the 700 ton coaster, H8, which was the transport Van Grieken had used on his journies between Guernsey and St. Malo. Considerable damage was done to buildings in the region of the harbour and windows were blown in as far away as the Bordage and Mill Street. The Town Church was so badly damaged it could not be used for divine service for nearly nine months.

The next day the Dutchman went to the harbour and, to his surprise, found the ship in which he had travelled sunk at its moorings against the quay. Astonishingly there were no guards on the ship and he was able to see the sunken vessel was totally abandoned. Later he discovered the raid had cost the lives of 31 slave workers, who had been unloading the cargo. The casualties were buried at the Foulon cemetery but the bodies were later exhumed and reburied in France. Despite the efforts of German salvage teams the ship remained sunk until the Royal Navy salvaged it in July 1945. As a result of this raid two carters who had been employed by the Germans to transport cargoes from the harbour refused to work there on the grounds the harbour was a danger area.

The reaction of the German authorities to this refusal on the part of the carters to work in the harbour was one of pained surprise. They issued a notice drawing the attention of the islanders to the fact that German sailors risked their lives protecting the ships bringing the necessities of life to the island and therefore Guernseymen had a duty to assist the Germans. They went on to accuse the carters of cowardice and warned that their action might result in an even greater shortage of supplies. If this were to happen, they went on, the islanders would have the cowards in their midst to thank for their hardships.

In another raid the store in which Van Grieken worked, and which had an anti-aircraft battery on the roof, was strafed by an Allied fighter aircraft. The battery was badly damaged, the gun crews sustaining heavy casualties. After the dead and wounded had been taken away the conscript workers went to look at the damage. They found a scene of carnage with bloodstains everywhere and bits of uniform clothing and helmets lying around.

By the middle of August 1944 the Allied advances in France were rapidly putting the islands in danger of becoming isolated from the mainland and the German occupying forces were left to ponder on the Allies next move. When the Allies took little or no action against the islands in the months following the invasion, apart from the occasional air raid, the Germans were forced to conclude General Jodl had been right and it was the intention of the Allies to bypass the islands and starve the garrisons into submission. Immediate action was needed to prevent this happening.

The first thing done was to get rid of all the remaining non-essential Organisation Todt workers. Those on Alderney, some 1,250 in all, were transferred to St. Malo while others were sent to Germany. Out of the original 18,000 O.T. workers less than one thousand remained, of which more than half were in Guernsey.

As the transports took the workers out they returned with munitions. The aim was to ensure the island garrisons had at least six months stock of everything they needed and extra shipping was made available to achieve this objective. However, it was a case of 'too little, too late.' It soon became evident that while the main islands could produce enough food to maintain the garrisons, the unproductive civilian populations would consume much of the fuel, flour and meat which would have to be brought in. The suggestion was made that the civilians should be evacuated and this idea was put to Hitler but the Führer seemed unable to make up his mind about this proposal.

By mid-August it was estimated the islands had only three months supply of food left and the German commanders were instructed to ruthlessly cut civilian food rations to ensure the survival of the German garrisons. A number of abortive attempts were made to supply the islands by air drop but these failed because of a shortage of equipment to perform the task. At the end of August the Germans were reduced to advising the British Government, through Switzerland acting as the protecting power, that 'on the former British Channel Islands supplies for the civilian population are exhausted.' The German Government indicated its willingness to allow all inhabitants, except men fit to serve in the armed forces, to be evacuated, or to allow food supplies to be sent to the islands for the support of the civilian population.

The reaction to this proposal in London was very much in favour of sending food supplies to the islands. The Chiefs of Staff were against evacuation as it would have tied up shipping needed elsewhere. The Home Office thought the idea of forcibly moving the islanders, after they had endured years of occupation, 'would be discouraging.' The General view was that the least that could be done for the islanders was to send them the necessities of life.

The Prime Minister, Winston Churchill, was violently opposed to any idea of sending food to the islanders. He was convinced, although proved totally wrong in the long term, that the German garrisons would seize any food sent in and leave the civilian population to starve. He wrote, in a minute, 'Let 'em starve. No fighting. They can rot at their leisure.'

Churchill had several changes of mind over the next few weeks. First he thought the idea of evacuation was the answer and refused to consider the sending in of food supplies. He then decided evacuation was not feasible and the German Government should be informed that, so long as their troops remained in occupation, they must be responsible for feeding the people. If the Germans indicated they were not going to accept this responsibility, they should surrender immediately. He did agree, finally, that if the Germans refused to take responsibility for feeding the civilian population, the Red Cross could be asked to send in food.

The decision of the British Government was passed from the Foreign Office, through the British Legation in Berne, to the German Foreign Ministry who immediately took the view that the British were about to exploit the situation to make the maximum propaganda value out of it. Their first reaction was to institute an enquiry into the precise situation regarding food supplies in the islands and also into the effect of evacuating the civilian population. The outcome of this investigation concluded the original claim that supplies for the civilian population were exhausted was not true, also that many of the civilian population were working for the Germans and could not be replaced by troops. The view of the German High Command was that if essential supplies for the civilian population were allowed in, via the International Red Cross, the garrisons would be able to hold out until, at least, the spring of 1945. Their aim was to be able to survive until the end of that year.

The diplomatic exchanges took so long to reach any conclusion meant the advances of the Allies in Europe had so totally isolated the islands that, with the Allies total command of both sea and air in the region, the Germans could no longer bring in supplies or evacuate any of the civilian population, surplus Organisation Todt men remaining in the islands, nor any non-effective troops. Those who were left had to stay. Gilbert Van Grieken and his fellow labourers, together with their German masters became, to all intents and purposes, prisoners of the Allies.

Before the state of seige had fully developed however, the Germans had one last blow to deliver. A party of five German POWs had managed to escape from an American prisoner of war camp at Granville and, after stealing an American landing craft, managed to reach St. Helier. They gave full details of the harbour activities at Granville, the strength of American troops in the area and the location of radar and signals units. Included in the information was the fact that most of the ships using the harbour at Granville were colliers and coal was badly needed in the Channel Islands.

The operation to attack the port, destroy installations and tow away a fully laden collier was only partly successful owing to the fact the Germans had miscalculated the tidal conditions in the harbour and three of the colliers they had targeted were firmly aground when they arrived. They were, nevertheless, able to do a considerable amount of damage to the port and returned to St. Helier with 30 prisoners and 55 German POWs who had been released. Subsequent reports suggest the German POWs were not exactly overwhelmed with gratitude at their release. Life in an American POW camp was, it would seem, preferable to joining a garrison under seige.

Towards the end of 1944 it dawned on the German commanders that they had the resources of manpower and land to grow considerable quantities of food to augment the rations available to the troops. The more the Germans could produced for themselves the less would be the impact of declining food stocks. Some of the troops had been growing vegetables as a way of filling in the many hours of tedious inactivity they were forced to endure and the troops manning the formidable 'Mirus' battery had even asked for permission to keep a cow on the site.

Unfortunately for the Germans they were not very efficient as market gardeners, nor could the process of growing be speeded up. Nevertheless desperate attempts were made to encourage food production by the troops. Each battalion was ordered to appoint an officer to be responsible for agriculture and quantities of seed potatoes were planted in requisitioned glasshouses. All this effort, however, was too late to affect the immediate food shortage.

Further attempts were made to supply the islands by air but these met with only limited success. Two Heinkel 111 bombers reached Guernsey in October and it was planned to send one each month but, in fact, no more supplies by air were received until the following February.

The diplomatic exchanges, which had started in early September 1944, between the British and German governments as to who should be responsible for feeding the civilian populations of the Channel Islands dragged on for three months or more. The last major shipment, of 500 tons, had been received in Guernsey on 31 July. Suggestions had been made that further supplies be brought in by U-boat but these were considered impractical as a U-boat could only carry supplies by the tens of tons whereas hundreds of tons were needed. Finally, after a lot of argument in London the British Government advised the German Government it was prepared to ask the International Red Cross to arrange a supply of food for the civilian population of the islands.

The German Government was not exactly eager to respond to this proposal. They spent almost two months examining the situation from every possible point of view and arguments about what supplies should be permitted bounced around from Ministry to Ministry. Eventually, on 23 November 1944, they notified the British Government that food parcels and medical supplies would be allowed into the Channel Islands. The International Red Cross would supervise the distribution of the parcels, and that their ships would be given safe conduct.

In the islands, meanwhile, the German commanders decided to requisition all civilian food stocks, despite violent objections raised by the civil authorities. The view of the Germans was that their primary duty lay in ensuring the garrisons could hold out as long as possible. They considered, since the British were committed to sending in food supplies for the civilian population, any other stocks should be reserved for the military. In addition to the food held by the islands civil authorities the Germans issued orders that all private stocks, over a small minimum were to be surrendered for military use. In Guernsey this order was backed up by a threat of a house to house search for non-compliance. This order, which amounted to legalised theft, brought some astonishing hoards to light. One man was found to have a stock of 363 tins of soup, vegetables and fish as well as 365 bottles of spirits. The Royal Hotel had to surrender 300 bottles of spirits and 360 tins of vegetables. The Germans justified these, and other seizures on the grounds that the civilian population should not expect to be better fed than the German troops and their auxiliaries, such as Gilbert Van Grieken and his fellow forced labourers for whom the Germans had to provide. While the Germans were no particularly concerned with the welfare of their unwilling guests, they were stuck with them so they had to be fed, even if only at subsistence level and this was about the level they had to endure in the coming months.

Chapter 9
THE LAST WINTER

As the year 1944 reached its close the attitudes of the protagonists towards the Channel Islands had settled into their final phases. The land battle in Europe had all but reached the borders of the German Reich. Italy had been overrun and large areas of France, Belgium and Holland liberated. In the east the Russian armies were crossing Poland and advancing fast into the German heartland.

As far as the British were concerned they had no intention of mounting a costly attack against the islands which they regarded as holding 30,000 German prisoners of war who they didn't even have to bother to guard. From the German point of view, while they must have known their cause was lost, could not face the dishonour of surrender in the light of the Führer's command that they hold out to the last. It was stalemate but the Allies were in no hurry since all the indications they had received suggested the islanders were, at worst, on tolerably friendly, if uncomfortable, relations with their occupiers. There was nothing to be gained by mounting an attack which would do more harm than good.

Admiral Kranke, given responsibility for maintaining the resistance of the island fortresses, tried to boost the morale of the garrisons at Christmas by arranging that relatives of the troops stationed there could send parcels to their menfolk. The difficulties of supply, however, made delivery impossible and all that reached the troops were 15,000 parcels containing chocolate and cigarettes, enough to provide one parcel for every two soldiers. Needless to say, nothing was provided for the remaining O. T. labour force.

For the civilian population conditions continued to deteriorate. Food and fuel were in desperately short supply with rations reduced to bare subsistence levels and these not always available. Supplies of tea were non existent, the weekly meat ration of three ounces was issued only once every four weeks and, owing to a lack of fuel and general deterioration of gear, fish became a very scarce commodity.

The fuel situation was equally desperate with gas strictly rationed and electricity supplies being cut off for several hours each day. Owing to a shortage of fuel to run the waterworks pumps the use of water was severely curtailed, orders being issued by the Germans, not really enforceable, that water was only to be used for drinking and cooking. A few days before Christmas the gas supply ceased altogether with the result, in those homes which relied on gas for cooking, that housewives had to cook as best they could on open fires. Fuel for fires was equally scarce, consisting mainly of wood from felled trees, when permission for felling could be obtained which was not always easy, or timbers from demolished glasshouses. Both sources of supply were strictly controlled with the result that many of the activities that would provide commodities like sugar, from sugar beet, and salt, from sea water, both requiring processing that needed heat, had to be halted, thus worsening the overall food supply situation.

Supplies of other commodities such as medical supplies and even mundane items like leather for repairing boots and shoes became equally critical. So bad had the overall supply situation become that the German commanders and the civil authorities spent a considerable time, to say nothing of a lot of effort, blaming each other for the shortages. Each claimed the other was responsible but all these acrimonious exchanges did nothing to alleviate the plight of the hungry and cold islanders.

The Germans were faring little better. One report describes their diet as consisting of sausages made from horse hides and soup made from potatoes, green vegetables and root vegetables. Dogs and cats had all but disappeared from Guernsey as the need for food, of any sort, became desperate. Thefts of food by German troops became endemic, houses were entered and several islanders wounded when they resisted German soldiers attempting to secure what food was in the house. Growing crops were ransacked in the fields and glasshouses to the extent that farmers and growers were compelled to harvest the crops before they were mature. One amusing story told is of a man watching his neighbour digging potatoes long before the crop would normally be considered ready for lifting. When asked what the crop was like the digger replied, "Not bad. I've got some as big as marbles, some as big as peas and a lot of little ones as well!"

Some relief for the civilian population finally came on 27 December, after the islanders had endured the bleakest Christmas of their lives. The Swedish ship *Vega* arrived in St. Peter Port carrying 100,000 food parcels donated by the Canadian and New Zealand Red Cross Societies and nearly 5,000 packages of medical supplies. Enough of the supplies were landed in Guernsey to provide a food parcel, containing around nine pounds of food, for every islander, man, woman and child, but with the warning that the contents would have to last them for a month before further supplies could be brought in. In addition to the food and medical supplies, salt, soap, tobacco and cigarettes were among the eagerly awaited stores. One surprising omission from the shipment was flour, a commodity the islands desperately needed. It was to take three months, many requests, and several more visits by the *Vega* before 150 tons of flour was to arrive and when it did there was some disappointment. The flour was of a type used in the making of puff pastry and not best suited for bread making. The resultant loaves lacked roughage with the consequence the bread caused severe constipation in many people who at it. In the absence of medicines to treat the condition the island's medical authorities were reduced to appealing for details of folk remedies which claimed to alleviate the ailment.

Small though the additional rations provided by the food parcels were, they made the difference between semi-starvation and subsistence. They also contributed greatly to the general health and welfare of the islanders. Not surprisingly, however, the issue of the parcels brought out the usual percentage of complaints that any such free gift generates. The bone of contention was the differing contents of the parcels. The Canadian parcels were fractionally larger than the New Zealand ones but contained less variety. The nutritional value of the contents of all the parcels was judged by experts to be equal but this did not stop those who were given one variety complaining the other was better. Such is human nature, there will always be the complainers. Perhaps it would have done some good to let them see the conditions in the Organisation Todt camps and try the food rations on which the slave workers had to exist.

The complaints, however, were of no concern to the Germans. Under the supervision of the Red Cross, distribution of the food parcels was confined to the civilian population and the German authorities made no attempt to interfere with this distribution. What they did was to increase their requisition of locally produced food, mainly vegetables and milk products. The Germans had previously decided that the cattle stocks in the island should be maintained to provide as much milk as possible, rather than slaughtering cattle to provide a bigger meat ration. As a result of this policy the cattle stock in Guernsey was at about the same level at the end of the occupation as at the beginning. Although the civilian population of the island was only about half its normal level, the presence of some 18,000 German troops, and their auxiliaries, resulted in stringent rationing of milk for the civilians. What milk they did get, with the exception for small babies, was skimmed, with a fat content of around 0.2%, as against the normal 4.5%, with the whole milk being used to manufacture butter and cheese to feed the German troops.

The Germans used the supply of food parcels as an excuse for their increased requisition of stocks, claiming the additional food provided, when added to the rations still available to the civilian population from island stores, represented an adequate diet. The German commandant was determined his troops should have at least the same, if not better, rations than the civilians. His task was to ensure the occupying troops would remain an efficient fighting force until, at last, the middle of 1945 and possibly beyond, until the hoped for change of German fortune in the war could bring them relief. It was a fairly hopeless objective since the supply of food available to the German troops was totally inadequate, by any accepted standards, to provide a diet necessary to meet the requirements to maintain operational troops in a fit state for combat duty.

Bad though conditions were, in terms of availability of food for the civilian population it is evident they could have been infinitely worse. Contemporary accounts of conditions vary widely, no doubt reflecting the writer's personal circumstances, but one written by Ralph Durand, published by the Guernsey Society in London in 1946, provides an extract from a diary kept by a member of a family of three in 1945: "March 6th. Breakfast: Radishes and stewed swedes. Dinner: Stewed swedes, the greater part of a 10 oz. tin of Canadian salmon, and cocoa. Afternoon tea: Substitute tea, jam spread on slices of boiled potatoes. Supper: Radishes, stewed swedes flavoured with sauce made from the remainder of the salmon."

Not exactly an inspiring diet but it must be noted that four meals were served in the day, a fact that does not indicate marked deprivation, and there is no suggestion in the narrative that this was an unusual day. The menu could, of course, be interpreted as an attempt to maintain, as much as possible, a normal life style in the face of adversity. This could well be the unwitting testimony passed down by the writer of the diary as he, or she, sought to explain how they managed to survive the final months of the occupation.

On the other hand, Gilbert Van Grieken and his fellow forced labourers, working in the German stores, were forced to supplement the slender rations given them by a little pilfering. One trick was to poke a small hole in a sack of wheat or sugar and transfer some of the contents to their pockets. If they were feeling particularly brave or desperate they would tie the wrist of a jacket sleeve and fill the sleeve with pilfered goods. Throwing the jacket over the shoulders, they would skylark among themselves as they walked past the guards on the way out of the warehouse, trusting the guard would not notice the stuffed sleeve. This, in fact, was the trick some of them had pulled on the day they were stopped in St. Julian's Avenue by the mysterious man, who spoke to them in Dutch, and the reason they had hurried away from him.

If the forced labourers were able to obtain some wheat by this means, they would pound the grains between two stones to make a form of coarse flour. With the flour, and some water, they made wheat cakes which were baked on the stove in their room. The Germans distributed a small amount of coal, enabling the labourers to heat their rooms, and this provided the cooking facility. The resultant wheat cakes were considered very good and, if chewed slowly, lasted quite a long time. They did, at last, provide some solid food to add to the never ending diet of watery soup.

In general, however, during the winter months of 1945 the food situation gradually deteriorated. Although the *Vega* returned each month it was a small ship with limited capacity, and on the last visit in April brought only a small amount of food, in addition to bales of clothing and footwear.

Of all the people in the island, the German soldiers were certainly the worst off and were reduced to fairly extensive rummaging and stealing to secure anything in the way of extra food to add to their meagre rations. Despite rigorous requisitioning of anything in the form of foodstuff that could be acquired from civilian sources the physical condition of many German troops deteriorated to the point they were no longer an effective fighting force. The rations they were given were only barely sufficient to support life if no work was done, so their duties had to be reduced to the minimum compatible with maintaining some sort of military efficiency. The working day of the soldiers was reduced to no more than five hours a day following which they were ordered to take two hours rest in order to conserve energy. Despite the earnest efforts of Vice Admiral Huffmeir, who had been appointed Admiral, Channel Islands in March 1945, to raise the morale of his troops by declaring his intention of holding the islands 'until final victory' it was obvious the end was in sight.

Word reached the island, on 1 May 1945, of the death of Adolf Hitler. The news was so widespread that even Gilbert Van Grieken heard about it, and both civilian and military were left for a few days to wonder what the German commanders would do.

As the next days passed excitement among the civilian population grew. They started to display openly the Union Jack while the German troops just stood by and watched. The soldiers accepted the war was lost and, in their weakened condition, were being careful not to do anything which might create animosity among the civilians but the same could not be said of their commanders. On 3 May a message was sent to Vice Admiral Huffmeir inviting him to surrender which met with the reply, on 6 May, that 'the Commander in Chief, Channel Islands receives orders only from his own government.'

The orders finally came on 7 May, after the German High Command had signed an unconditional surrender, and Huffmeir agreed to send a representative to meet Brigadier Snow, commander of the British forces, aboard HMS *Bulldog* off the Hanois. The representative, a junior naval officer, informed Brigadier Snow he had come aboard to discuss terms of an armistice and was smartly sent packing with the message there was no armistice, unconditional surrender were the terms. Before leaving the warship the German officer warned it was still only 8 May and if the British warships remained where they were would be fired on.

At length Vice Admiral Huffmeir gave in. He advised the British that his second in command, General Major Heine, would come aboard *Bulldog* and arrange for the surrender. Heine came aboard after midnight on 8 May and agreed there would be a ceasefire from one minute past midnight on 9 May. *Bulldog* moved to St. Peter Port, where Heine signed the instrument of surrender at dawn. Liberation had come after nearly five weary years.

Chapter 10
LIBERATION AND A NEW LIFE

Liberation came to Gilbert Van Grieken in the shape of a British soldier pointing a Sten gun at him. Had he but known it, young Gilbert was probably more at danger of death or injury at that moment than at any time during the war, even when the German SS officer with wobbly legs had held a Luger pistol to his head. The Sten gun, a British wartime production, designed for cheap, easy mass production, intended to use the millions of rounds of Italian 9mm parabellum ammunition captured during the 1940 campaigns in Libya, was without doubt the most inherently dangerous weapon every produced in Britain. Its design broker every safety rule laid down over the centuries by the Ordnance Board, it was of crude construction, without proper safety devices, and required only a sharp knock to set it firing inadvertently. It was not a weapon one would want to face.

The incident occurred when Van Grieken was walking across the top of the Gibauderie and he came across a group of women talking to the soldier. The women pointed to the Dutchman, undoubtedly telling the solder "That's one of them" and, as Van Grieken drew close, the soldier told him to stop. Pointing his Sten gun at the hapless youth he demanded to known who he was and what was his business.

Fortunately this time, probably having learned his lesson in Amsterdam five years earlier when the lack of identity papers earned him three hours in police custody, the young Dutchman was carrying identification papers, including his Dutch passport. Showing his papers to the soldier he was able to convince this representative of the British liberating force he was not a German soldier in disguise but a forced labourer, of Dutch nationality, brought to the island by the German authorities. The soldier, satisfied with this explanation, wished the Dutchman good luck and let him go on his way.

Going down into the town, towards the harbour, Van Grieken was joined by some of his fellow workers. They marvelled at the sight of hundreds of people milling around. Flags were flying from almost every building and the harbour, where no shops had been seen for many a month, was filled with shipping. There was merriment everywhere but, as much as the forced labourers enjoyed the celebrations, their gaiety was marred by the realisation they no longer had anybody to house and feed them. They seemed to have been left to their own resources. The group of conscript labourers sombrely returned to their quarters and discussed their situation. A supply of food seemed to be the first priority so they went to see the commander of the German unit at the girls grammar school to enquire how they were going to be fed in future. The commander appeared to be very drunk but he listened to their problem then wrote something on a piece of paper and told them to take it to the store. At the store the store man gave them each a loaf of bread, some butter and a few tins of meat. Their immediate needs were thus met.

The action of the women in pointing out the Dutchman to the British soldier was symbolic of the time. Many an old score was settled by worthy citizens denouncing others as collaborators, black marketeers, hoarders of food and so on. Intelligence officers of the liberating force, which was in effect a military government empowered by the Defence (Channel Islands) Regulations, 1944, to take over from the civil authorities responsibility for essential supplies, communications, dealing with cases of assisting the enemy, sabotage, movement of persons, public safety and order, interrogated hundreds of prisoners of war, the few remaining political prisoners and Organisation Todt workers in an attempt to identify war criminals. A great deal of time of the officers of the civil affairs unit was wasted in taking statements from inhabitants who were of the opinion that some of their fellow islanders had gone out of their way to give assistance to the Germans. When all the evidence had been sifted much of it was found to be based on hearsay and suspicion, offering nothing like the standard of evidence necessary to support a charge of treason or treachery. In the end it was decided there were no grounds for criminal prosecution and the subject of collaborators was dropped, much to the annoyance of some.

Nobody bothered to question Gilbert Van Grieken about any atrocity he might have seen, although he had witnessed some. One incident took place near the Royal Hotel where some French slave labourers were working on the light railway line the Germans had installed to move materials from the harbour to the gun emplacement building sites. One of the Frenchmen struck an O.T. guard who promptly seized a long handled shovel and used it to beat his attacker to death. On another occasion, walking down Pedvin Street, where the houses were being used as billets for slave workers, Van Grieken saw a lorry parked by one house. On the pavement beside the lorry was a crude wooden box. As the Dutchman, and his Guernseyman companion, walked past, some slave workers together with an O.T. guard came out of the house carrying a body wrapped in a blanket. The slave workers put the body in the box, which was too small to take it. The O.T. guard stamped on the body with his jackboots, as if to try to force it into the box. Van

Grieken and his friend did not stop to see what was happening. They knew better than to offend an O.T. guard, so they hurried away from the scene.

Horrendous tales of atrocity came from Alderney, where it was claimed many hundreds of slave workers and concentration camp inmates had been killed. One man, who had remained on the island doing agricultural work for the Germans, claimed he had recorded the burial of 1,000 of these victims of Nazi brutality. So vivid and detailed were the stories that a special investigation team was sent to the island to enquire into the allegations. While the investigators found the remains of a concentration camp, the buildings having been burned down, and evidence of brutally inhumane treatment of O.T. workers and concentration camp inmates, there was no evidence of any mass graves or wholesale slaughter. When pressed, the individual claiming knowledge of the thousand burials could not produce any evidence to the investigators and it seems likely his story was concocted for him to feed to an eager press forever seeking new, and preferably lurid, stories. The investigators did find some meticulously kept records of death certificates and came to the conclusion that the number of slave workers and prisoners who died in Alderney was 337.

One of the stories told was that the bodies of slave workers, and concentration camp inmates, who had been shot were dumped in the setting concrete of the gun bunkers and sealed there forever. Unfortunately for the tellers, this story had long ceased to have credence as it was one that started life in the Hollywood movies of the 1930's, when it was portrayed as the favourite means of disposal by gangsters of the bodies of their victims. The same story has been told time and time again, the last time it emerged was in the late 1960' when it was claimed the bodies of those slain in London gangland wars were buried in the concrete pillars of the elevated section of the M4 motorway in London.

However, despite the pointing fingers in Guernsey, and the round up and interrogation by the military authorities of German troops and auxiliaries, nobody seemed to have any interest in the welfare of Gilbert Van Grieken. Left to his own devices, and deprived of the 'protection' of his German masters, he was forced to seek his own salvation and find food and shelter where he could.

Fortunately for him, during the occupation he had made friends with a young Guernseyman of similar age, Geoff Lowe, who lived with his family in Stanley Road. The two young men had amused themselves trying to teach the other their own languages and exchanged bits of food whenever they had any to spare. The Lowe family, having an unused room in their house, viewed with sympathy the plight of the young Dutchman and took him in while he looked for some form of work or could find his way home to Holland. He at least was not penniless as he had entrusted Geoff Lowe with nearly 1,000 Reichmarks, savings from his wages, which had been placed in a bank account. After the Liberation, Mr Lowe had gone to the bank, transferred the money to an account in the name of Gilbert Van Grieken, and presented the Dutchman with a bankbook showing him to have £100 to his credit.

To deal with the food problem Van Grieken went to the States Office and obtained a ration card which entitled him to buy rations as a civilian and, to his surprise, he was also given a Red Cross food parcel. He was a little surprised the Germans had not distributed these parcels to their workers but he was not to know the Red Cross representatives in the island had made sure German hands had been kept off these life saving supplies.

Wandering around the town one day he met a British sailor and explained he was trying to find work. Did the sailor know of any to be had? The sailor did. He was a Royal Navy mess steward, based at the Royal Hotel looking after naval officers staying there. He told the Dutchman the manager was looking for waiters, an opportunity which was rapidly explored.

The manager of the Royal Hotel, a Mr. Manning who ran the hotel with the assistance of his daughter, was clearly impressed with the young applicant as he took him on and told him he could start work the next day. Fitted out with a waiter's uniform and given a staff room in the hotel Gilbert Van Grieken's immediate problems were, for the moment, solved.

The hotel was mainly occupied by bankers and members of the Civil Affairs Unit who had come to advise the Military Government on action to be taken in the transition back from occupation to civil rule. In fact they had little to do as the civil authority in the island had remained intact throughout the occupation and the main task revolved around the financial problems caused by the occupation costs and the introduction into the island of German occupation Reichmarks as an alternative currency. This currency was now valueless but something had to be done about it otherwise the holders would be left to bear much of the costs of the occupation. In the end the States decided to redeem the Reichmarks by converting them into Sterling and the British Government made a substantial contribution to cover the cost. There were other minor problems to be dealt with. Any laws or ordinances passed by the States during the occupation were invalid as their authority to pass these measures had, unknown to the Bailiff or States, been revoked by Order in Council. All these problems were, however, soon resolved and the Military Government ceased to function on 25 August 1945. A new Lieutenant Governor was appointed and the island restored to its normal civil administration.

While he was content enough with his job as a waiter, Van Grieken still dreamed of the day he could go home and take up his trade as a carpenter. He did not know that, as yet, the Dutch authorities were not ready to take back the many thousands of their nationals who had been conscripted by the Germans. They had problems of their own and, in fact, the repatriation of Dutch conscripts was not to be completed until April 1946, nearly a year after the end of the war. In the meantime the young Dutchman got on with his job, which had its compensations.

One day an American bank official who he had served on several occasions gave him a handful of coins which amounted to nearly three pounds, the equivalent of a week's wages in those days, explaining he was leaving the next day and had no further use for the money. Some guests in the hotel were quite generous with their tips, others were not so forthcoming. Among the latter group was the Bailiff, Sir Victor Carey, who considered the service charge was enough. Tips were the cause of a quarrel between Van Grieken and the other waiter in the dining room, an Italian, who told the Dutchman they should share any tips received. Van Grieken noticed the Italian rarely received any tips and, in any case, he did not trust his colleague, so he refused. The Italian became somewhat belligerent and Van Grieken took good care to avoid him as much as possible.

After he had worked at the Royal Hotel for about five months the Dutch Consul, Mr. Prins, told him that arrangements had been made for him to return home. This news upset Mr. Manning, who wanted the Dutchman to stay and offered to make all the necessary arrangements with the authorities for a permit, but the young man wanted to go home and declined the offer.

The arrangements made for the repatriation of Van Grieken, and other former conscript workers, appear to have been co-ordinated by the French Consul, M. Lambert. Instructions were given to the Dutch by Mr. Prins, who gave each worker a pair of Netherlands army boots, (they thought as a present from their government but some of them later received a bill for the equivalent of £3.50 for the boots), to report to M. Lambert at the harbour. They were further instructed to hand over to M. Lambert any occupation Reichmarks they had in their possession and an equal sum in Dutch Guilders would be given them when they reached home. Van Grieken had a fair sum, given to him by the O.T. paymaster at the end of the occupation as wages owing to him, and duly handed it over. That was the last he was to see of it, or of the Guilders into which it was supposed to be converted. He often wonders what became of his Reichmarks but, at least, he was not one of those who received a bill for the boots, that was some benefit!

On the appointed day, in late September 1945, the repatriates said goodbye to their friends and assembled at the White Rock. With their mixed attire, clutching bundles and assorted hand baggage, they looked for all the world like nineteenth century European emigrants setting off for the New World.

They almost didn't believe their eyes when they saw the ship that was to take them on the first stage of their journey home. The vessel which awaited them had started life as a Dutch Rhine river barge but had been modified, by removal of the bow section, and converted into a landing craft. Several hundred of these barges had been confiscated in Holland and used around the coasts of Europe as supply vessels. The captain of the repatriate's transport had been a Russian soldier, an ex prisoner of war found in Guernsey who was later allowed to settle in the island, presumably in recognition of the services he had rendered to the community by taking his ship to France, on a number of occasions, to bring back cargoes of food and other essential commodities. The passengers were made to sit on the top of the deck of the vessel and were warned not to move around. There were no railings around the deck to protect the travellers from falling overboard so it was fortunate the weather for the trip was calm. Only a gentle swell, created by a slight breeze, disturbed the surface of the sea as the converted barge made its way very slowly from St Peter Port to Granville, a journey which took about five hours. Although the passengers were spared the unpleasant experience of seasickness on an overcrowded vessel with no protection from the elements they thought, had the journey lasted much longer, that they might soon succumb from the effects of the gentle, but continuous, up and down movement of the ship.

In addition to the group of Dutchmen travelling home, the barge carried a number of Frenchmen and six French girls who had been working in a German army brothel in Hauteville. There can be little doubt these girls worked hard for their living as can be witnessed by a story told of the experiences of a bank manager. This worthy official of the bank had reported to the Controlling Committee that certain of the girls were depositing large sums in Occupation Reichmarks into their accounts at his bank. The Committee were concerned that the girls might be taking money from the German soldiers with the intention of converting the Reichmarks into convertable currency when the war was over then repaying the money to the Germans. The bank manager was told to investigate so he took himself off to the house of ill fame to discuss the matter with the Madam. He was somewhat taken aback when, after explaining his cause for concern about the substantial sums being deposited by the girls, he was told "You must understand, Monsieur, a good girl can service 25 to 30 men a day. Their earnings can be very high." The embarrassed bank manager retired to pass on this message to the Controlling Committee.

Eventually the barge reached Granville, but if the passengers expected a civic welcome they were in for a nasty surprise. On the dockside some 24 French soldiers, dressed in ill fitting British army uniforms and looking dirty and unshaven, were waiting. Their attitude towards the repatriates was far from friendly as they roughly herded their charges into buses and took them to a half derelict hotel. The end of the street where the hotel was situated had been barricaded off and behind the barricade a crowd of several hundred French civilians were seen shouting abuse at the new arrivals.

The abuse of the civilians was matched by the French speaking repatriates who returned the insults, accompanied by 'V' signs with their fingers and the shouting of slogans like "Heil Churchill" and "Vive la France." Some of the other repatriates taunted the civilians by fooling about and dancing in the street. All these activities only served to further infuriate the French civilians, who presumably thought the party brought to the hotel were captured collaborators, and one woman tried to scale the barricade, with the clear aim of inflicting some injury, but she was driven back by one of the soldiers. Nevertheless the tumult didn't die down until the repatriates were safely inside the hotel.

Once inside the hotel interrogations started, conducted by French officers most of whom spoke no language other than their own. The records of interrogation caused the repatriates, at least the non-French speaking ones, some concern as it seemed the officers were simply writing down whatever they thought the repatriates had told them, right or wrong. The interrogation was followed by an examination of baggage and at this point Gilbert Van Grieken found himself in a spot of bother. When he opened his case the French soldier conducting the examination found a number of tins of food from Red Cross food parcels, which the Dutchman had carefully saved as presents for his family, and accused him of smuggling food. The food, the soldier said, would be confiscated.

Van Grieken's reaction to this proposal was outrage and he told the

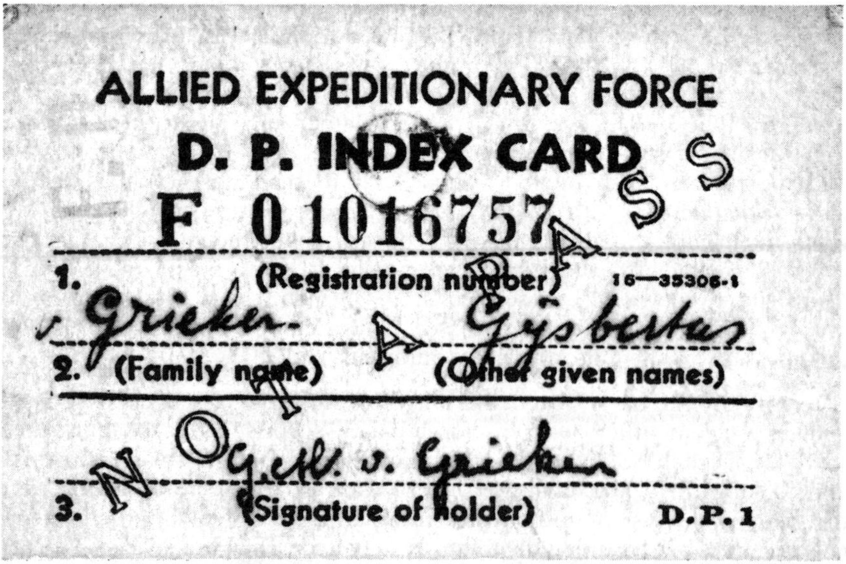

ALLIED EXPEDITIONARY FORCE

D. P. INDEX CARD

F 01016757

1. (Registration number) 16—35306-1

v. Grieken Gysbertus

2. (Family name) (Other given names)

G.W. v. Grieken

3. (Signature of holder) D.P.1

Displaced Persons Registration Card issued to Gilbert Van Grieken in France — 1945

Frenchman, in no uncertain terms, to take his dirty fingers off his property. He closed his case and made to walk off. The French soldier ordered him to stay where he was, while he fetched an officer to deal with the situation. Fortunately for the Dutchman a fellow Dutch national, a Rotterdam crane driver, had heard the exchange and said "Gilbert, give me your case and you have mine. We can change them back later." The exchange was swiftly made, before the soldier returned with the officer.

The French officer ordered Van Grieken to open his case and found it contained only dirty clothes and a couple of tins of food. This the officer thought not unreasonable and became very abusive to the soldier. "Is this what you called me for?" he asked. "Let this man go on his way with his few tins of food and do not waste my time any more." The Dutchman sped off, as fast as his feet would carry him, to find his crane driver friend. The two had a hearty laugh at the soldier's discomfort as they exchanged cases again.

The repatriates were left that night to sleep on the floor, no beds or blankets being provided. Neither was food or drink made available and the men spent the night moaning, some expressing the opinion they were better off under the Germans. Sleep does not come easily when the only bed available is a hard floorboard.

At about 8 a.m. the following morning the repatriates were once again herded on to buses and driven to the railway station, escorted by the French soldiers. They were put on a train for Paris and the military escort then left them to their own devices. During the journey Gilbert Van Grieken was able to see, for the first time, the terrible damage done during the closing stages of the war. Blown bridges, wrecked stations, rolling stock, broken and burned out, lying beside the track. Everywhere the ravages of total war were to be seen.

The train arrived in Paris at 2 p.m. and, again, buses were waiting to take the men to a huge stadium with buildings alongside, which looked like schools. As each man entered he was given a parcel containing soap, toothbrush, toothpaste, shaving soap and a new towel. They were then led to long tables set out for a meal and told to sit down. It was announced that each nationality had to sing their own national anthem and this they did with gusto, in fervent gratitude for the fact they were, once again, free men. After the singing, which lasted about 20 minutes, a substantial meal was served. It was also announced that each man could obtain from the canteen, during the evening, two glasses of beer, free of charge. After the hostile reception they had received at Granville the repatriates opinion of the French took a distinct turn for the better at this treatment. To them the atmosphere of the place was like a holiday camp.

After three days at the stadium the repatriates were moved again, this time to a Canadian army camp where they were accommodated in tents, 12 men to a tent. Van Grieken managed to find room in the same tent as his crane driver friend from Rotterdam and had time to notice the camp contained several thousand people who had been recovered from many parts of Europe. They were the strangest collection of human flotsam ever seen. Their dress was, to say the least, somewhat bizarre and uniformly shabby. One man was wearing a German army jacket and jackboots, he explained that when the war ended he had no decent clothes so he, and some others, had raided a German army clothing store to fit themselves out with wearable apparel.

At this camp the Dutch national repatriates were interrogated by members of the Dutch army Princess Irene Brigade. The Dutch military wanted to find out how and why the Dutchmen were working for the Germans. Although the individual interrogations did not last long, only about 10 minutes, they were intense and intended to ensure the returning forced labourers did not have time to invent what they might have thought a suitable story. The men were led in groups of three into an interrogation room where they faced a five member military team. The five interrogators fired questions in rapid succession at the repatriates. Van Grieken was asked if he had ever been a member of the NSB (Netherlands National Socialist Commission). He said he had not.

Then he was asked to explain how he had come to work for the Germans. This question he answered with the story of his direction, by the Amsterdam Labour Office in 1940, to report for work in Germany and his subsequent orders, from the same office, to work for the Organisation Todt. His answers were carefully noted down and, presumably being satisfactory, he was told he was free to occupy his time in any way he liked while he remained at the camp.

Once through the interrogation process the repatriates were left to their own devices, for the remaining days of their two week stay. They were able to visit Paris, having been given some money and they were able to further supplement their funds by selling their cigarette ration to the French. These outings made a pleasant change from the camp, although even in the camp the atmosphere was very light hearted.

The men, now officially recognised as Displaced Persons and given identity cards denoting this status, made their own amusement by playing practical jokes on each other. One night Van Grieken was asleep in his tent when he found himself being pulled off his palliasse by his legs and was dragged, yelling and screaming, several yards down a pathway. His assailants, laughing like maniacs, dropped his legs and ran off into the night. He never found out who they were but he had his suspicions. The whole affair was regarded by the other occupants of the tent as a huge joke.

On another occasion a group of the men went swimming in a nearby gravel pit and the young Gilbert was foolish enough to tell the others he was afraid he was going to lose his trunks, which were only held up with some box cord. A couple of the lads swam over to him and pulled his trunks off, then swam ashore telling him if he wanted his trunks he would have to come out of the water to get them. This situation caused a great deal of amusement among a group of Dutch girls, sunning themselves nearby, and they took part in the catcalls which accompanied the young man's embarrasment. Finally his tormenters relented and threw back his trunks. The mixed audience thought it a great joke, but not poor Gilbert.

Eventually the Dutch contingent in the camp were told they would be moved again, this time home, but nobody knew their exact destination. They were given rations of bread and tinned meat to last them for the journey and taken, by bus, to the Paris Gard du Nord railway station. The journey to Holland was excrutiatingly slow, the train frequently stopping and travelling very slowly over emergency bridges, so that 10 hours elapsed before it finally reached its destination, Eindhoven.

The Holland Gilbert Van Grieken returned to was in a state of confusion. Although the southern half of the country had been liberated by the advancing Allied armies in 1944 the Germans held on to the northern half, containing most of the major towns, until their surrender in May 1945. The destruction they wrought was extensive and included the flooding of the most fertile areas of land, destroying much of the capability of the Dutch to feed themselves. Much of the country's communications, especially bridges, had been destroyed by the enemy and many towns had suffered greviously from the effects of close hand-to-hand fighting and the destructive nature of tank warfare.

Not only was the country in economic chaos but also in political turmoil. Conforming to promises made early in the war, as soon as the Netherlands were liberated from German occupation, the government in exile resigned and a search was started for a new leader who would be acceptable to all political parties. This was not to prove easy. There was no parliament and the organisation of elections had been rendered almost impossible because the Resistance Movement had destroyed many of the central registries in the towns, to make the German's problems of government more difficult; people had moved about the country to avoid the areas flooded by the Germans and some had even moved into Belgium and France. The best that could be done, under the circumstances, was to form an emergency parliament from such members of the previous parliament still surviving, and who had been found free of collaborationist activities, plus a few members nominated by the now powerful Resistance Movement.

On all sides suspicion and mistrust were evident. Accusations of collaboration flew freely, much as they had in Guernsey immediately after the liberation, and the first thing the returning forced labourers had to do was to convince the several elements of Dutch authority, all of whom wanted a piece of the action, that they were free of any taint of collaboration.

On arrival at Eindhoven the travellers were transported by lorry to the Phillips factory where they were alloted sleeping accommodation, again simply a straw filled palliasse on the floor. They were then taken to a huge room, about 100 metres square, on the first floor where already some hundreds of people, both men and women, were milling about. Some appeared to be couples, having a row about something or other. Finally all the people were lined up and given a meal of bread and soup before returning to their sleeping accommodation, where they sat around chatting about affairs in general and swapping experiences.

The next morning it was announced over a public address system that when an individual's name was called out, that person had to present themselves for interrogation by the Royal Dutch Marechaussée. This body is an elite paramilitary police force responsible for internal security and its members are to be found at all harbours, airports and border crossings. They have very extensive powers, far greater, for example, than the ordinary police whose powers are limited to their own parish or town, or even those of the *Rijks Veldwachter* — the national police force. The Marechaussée are hand picked, extremely fit young men of good education and high intelligence.

The prospect of facing interrogation by this all powerful police force was not one that Gilbert Van Grieken particularly fancied. Although he had nothing to hide, as far as he knew, there was no telling what interpretations would be put on his actions. All he knew, from the reputation of the Marechaussée, was that if you tried to get away with anything you needed to be very clever indeed. Names were called out and people went for interrogation. As they returned they were quizzed by those awaiting their turn, but the general opinion among those who had been processed was that the police were very polite but strict and all said the interrogators could sense whether they were being told the truth. The opinion was voiced the Marechaussée could smell out wrong-doers!

In the party of returning forced labourers was another young man who had also been in Guernsey, working in the O.T. kitchens at Amherst School. One evening the young man, Toni Burks, came over to Van Grieken and sat on his palliasse to have a talk. He appeared very worried about something. "What is the matter, Toni," asked Van Grieken. "Come out with it. You must come clean if you want me to help you."

Toni had a bundle of photographs of himself and the O.T. men in Guernsey and was afraid if they were found on him he would be thought a collaborator. He asked Van Grieken if he would hold them for him, or should he destroy them. Van Grieken advised against destroying the photographs and agreed to look after them for his compatriot until after he had been interrogated. Having made that arrangement, Toni Burks admitted he had another problem. He said he had been in the Dutch army in 1940. His unit was engaged in combat with the Germans near Rotterdam. About half a day before the capitulation he had left his comrades and gone home to his parents in

Rotterdam. Now he was afraid he would be listed as a deserter and arrested by the Marechaussée, to be tried by Court Martial, for, as he put it, "a deserter is never forgotten."

A few hours later Burks' name was called and, after about a half hour, he returned to Van Grieken looking very worried. Questioned about his military record, he had told the interrogators what had happened in 1940. He had, he told them, been advised by his officer that the war for them was over. As he lived close by he could go home, otherwise he would end up in a prison camp with the rest of them. He had taken his officer's advice and gone home. The Marechaussée interrogators evidently thought this a strange story but not so improbable as to be necessarily untrue. They had warned Burks his story would be investigated further.

By evening, when his name had still not been called, Van Grieken suggested to Burks that they go for a walk in Eindhoven so they went to the gatehouse to get a pass out. Burks went in first, gave his name but was refused a pass. Then Van Grieken gave his name and, after consulting a list, the guard gave him a pass. This seemed strange to Van Grieken. Toni Burks who had been interrogated and released was refused a pass but he, who had not been seen by the Marechaussée, was allowed out. Anyway, having been given a pass Van Grieken decided to go for a walk on his own but found the town dead. He went into a bar and bought a glass of beer, which he found very enjoyable, then returned to the factory. On the way in he asked the guard why he had been able to get a pass when Burks had been refused. The reason, the guard told him, if your name is not on the suspect list so you are free to come and go as you please. It is quite likely you will not be called for interrogation. So it turned out. Van Grieken's name was never called and he is still very proud of the fact that, of all the people he spoke to, he was the only one who had been, at all times, free to go out of the gate whenever he chose. Van Grieken lost touch with his friend after they left Eindhoven but he heard later that when Toni Burks reached his home in Rotterdam he was arrested and held in custody for two weeks before being released. Van Grieken thought Burks was lucky but it is likely the Marechaussée, or the military authorities found his story was true. Feared, as they are, in Holland because of their diligence in the performance of their duties, the Marechaussée, as are all police in Holland, are scrupulously fair and if the young man's story of being told to go home proved true, they would not try to make it otherwise. In any case the Marechaussée, in the autumn of 1945, were probably far more concerned with tracking down the 80,000 plus Dutch citizens who, thinking they were jumping on the winning German bandwagon in 1940 and 1941, eagerly joined the Dutch National Socialist Movement. They will also have been on the lookout for survivors of the 25,000 Dutchmen who volunteered to form units of the German army to fight the Russians.

After being held in Eindhoven for about two weeks the repatriates were told they would, at last, be transported to their home towns. Once again the journey was painfully slow and, owing to the badly damaged state of the Dutch railway system, it was by a very circuitous route. The train meandered slowly via Arnhem, Utrecht and Amersfoort with the passengers for Rotterdam changing trains at Utrecht and those for Amsterdam being told they would have to stay the night at Amersfoort before completing their journey the next day.

Some three hours travelling brought the train to Arnhem but it stopped several hundred metres from the station and the passengers were told to disembark and walk to the station as the train could go no further. This instruction, which meant they had to carry their cases and bundles along the rough track side, generated a considerable amount of moaning from the passengers, but walk they did. Reaching the station they found another train which took them to Utrecht, where the Rotterdam passengers left the train after saying farewells to those remaining and expressing hopes for future meetings.

On to Amersfoort, the train moving slowly, especially across pontoon bridges thrown across rivers and streams. Finally arriving at their destination the passengers were taken by bus to a location which, much to their surprise, was a camp of several hundred wooden huts surrounded by barbed wire. What cheered them, however, was a large white banner stretched across the entrance with the message "WELKOM THUIS" — (Welcome Home) emblazoned across it.

On arrival at the camp the passengers were first taken to a large hut, where again a big welcome banner was displayed, and given a substantial meal. The meal consisted of soup, a main course garnished with carrots and peas and followed by a pudding. After the meal there was coffee but no singing of the national anthem, as in Paris, however the noise level of the conversation reached almost deafening proportions.

Once the meal was over the men were shown where they were to sleep for the night but since it was still early evening a few of them, including Gilbert Van Grieken, decided to explore their surroundings. They soon found out they were in a former concentration camp, still half full of SS prisoners of war and other Germans awaiting trial for war crimes. Somebody said "Go and have a look at that cage and you can see the 'Beul van Amersfoort' (Butcher of Amersfoort)." In the cage was an evil looking man dressed in officers uniform but with no rank badges or buttons. He had been deprived of braces so had to hold his trousers up and his boots had been replaced with wooden Dutch clogs. This man had been the Commandant of the concentration camp.

The cage, made of wire netting, measuring some 20 metres by 5 metres, was the exercise area for the prisoner, who walked up and down looking straight ahead all the time. After a while a crowd of several hundred had gathered and started hurling abuse but the German made no response. One man stood at the end of the cage and shouted

"Do you remember me? My name is . . . . . . and you ill-treated me when I was in this camp." He then ran backwards and forwards to alternate ends of the cage about six times, repeating this performance. The German took no notice, he just kept on walking up and down his cage. There was not a Dutch guard in sight but the prisoner was unlikely to escape, dressed as he was with a convict haircut. One of the onlookers expressed sorrow for the German saying, "We should not treat even our enemies like this." Another remarked, "If this is the worst we do to our enemies and war criminals they will not have much to complain about." Van Grieken agreed with the latter sentiment and said so. The group finally drifted away to their sleeping quarters and luxuriated in sleeping between clean sheets, on a mattress and camp bed. They had not known such comfort for many weeks.

The next morning they were off to Amsterdam, arriving about mid-day. Here the welcome was not so amiable. The travellers were guided into a big room and interrogated by the civil police to prove their identities and check on whether they had a criminal record. Van Grieken was one of a group of about 50 who were considered 'clean' and were given papers with instructions as to what they must do when they reached home. First they had to report to their own family doctor for a medical examination, then to the local police station for a further identification check and finally to the local Resistance group for political clearance, before a ration card would be issued.

After being cleared by the civil police the, by now weary, travellers were loaded into jeeps driven by Dutch army girls and taken to their homes. When Gilbert Van Grieken arrived home he found both his parents were out but a younger brother and sister were there to welcome him. After a joyous reunion his sister said, in sorrow, "We have no food to give you, Gilbert. Everything is still on coupons. We had better wait until Mother and Father come home. They will know what to do."

"Don't worry," answered Gilbert as he opened his suitcase containing a stock of Red Cross tins of food left over from his time in Guernsey and specially saved for this reunion. The two young children could hardly believe what they saw. "We haven't seen anything like this for years," they cried, so Gilbert opened some tins and had a meal with his brother and sister. "This is the best meal we have had since the Germans came," they said and Gilbert remembered they had been through the 'hunger winter' of 1944-1945. While the feast was in progress neighbours who had heard Gilbert was home hung out flags in celebration so that when his parents came home they found the street in festive mood. They, too, celebrated the safe return of their son with a meal of Red Cross food and the joy of the family at this reunion was complete.

The next norning life was back to normal, the flags were gone and Van Grieken was brought down to earth in the knowledge he had to face the hard facts of life, to complete his arrival procedure and try to find work. He visited the doctor, who pronounced him fit, then went to the police station. The policeman at the desk simply asked "What name?" Being given it he stamped the requisite form. The returning traveller thanked the police officer and left the station.

Van Grieken's encounter with the Resistance group was not so easy or pleasant. Having appointed themselves as Holland's conscience, fighting the influence of Nazi sympathisers and the authority of the German occupation authorities, they were reluctant to hand over to a statuary civil authority they could not legally oppose. They considered it their right to purge the nation of any collaborationist elements they could identify and went about their task with fervent, almost religious, zeal. The captain to whom Van Grieken reported was an ex-policeman who had previously been dismissed from the force for misconduct. As a captain in the Resistance he wielded a great deal of power and influence, to a degree far in excess of that he would ever have gained as a police constable, and he clearly enjoyed his new found authority.

Van Grieken put his form on the table and asked "Can you stamp this, please, so I can go and fetch my ration card?"

"Not so fast, not so fast my boy," answered the captain. "I see you are Gilbert Van Grieken. Have you any brothers and sisters?"

"Oh, yes. Several of them."

"Where are they now?" demanded the captain.

"I don't know," said Van Grieken. "Two of them are still in Germany, as far as I know, and one is in the Resistance. I only came home yesterday and have only seen my parents and a younger brother and sister. But, excuse me, Sir, why all this? I came here for a stamp for myself, not for my brothers and sisters. If there was anything wrong about them I could not tell you at this time, certainly not until I had found out about it from themselves."

The captain acted like the German in the cage, he said nothing and just sat and stared at the form on the desk. Finally, without a word, he stamped the form and, with a distinctly nasty look on his face, pushed it across the table. Van Grieken later discovered he had been on very dangerous ground arguing with the Resistance man who, if he felt the young man was being uncooperative or even plain cheeky, could have ordered him to be kept in custody for 'further investigation.'

However, with his form duly stamped, Van Grieken thanked the captain and took his leave, not altogether sure he was as free a man as he once thought. Outside the office stood a NBS soldier with his blue boiler suit, black helmet and a Sten gun, not an altogether comforting symbol of a society supposed to be liberated from the oppression of military occupation.

The task of reconstruction had barely got under way when Gilbert Van Grieken reached home and, although a vast amount of work needed to be done, the means to mobilise the work force and organise the reconstruction effort had yet to be found. The task of the interim government was not made easier by the Resistance Movement demanding a rigid purge of alleged collaborators which meant that tens of thousands of people were detained for interrogation, and trial when the charges against them looked valid. The post occupation pointing of fingers encouraged by suspicion, rumour, hatred and jealousy was by no means confined to Guernsey. Old scores were being settled by this means throughout Europe in the latter part of 1945. This might explain why Van Grieken was forced to endure lengthy and frequent interrogations as he made his way home.

To add to the problems of the Dutch government, in late 1945, many thousands of Dutch nationals previously living in the Netherlands East Indies were being driven back to Holland by the emergence of nationalist movements in those territories after the collapse of Japan. The arrival of these repatriates made further heavy demands on the limited housing and land space available in an already overcrowded country.

In addition to the shortage of food, fuel, clothing, raw materials and housing the Dutch government had to cope with the almost total destruction of the nation's earning capacity. Many of the factories and other production plants had been ruthlessly plundered by the Germans who had left literally nothing but bare walls. Machinery, machine tools and any removable equipment had been transported to Germany to aid their war effort. The Netherlands had been stripped bare.

Against this unhopeful background, Gilbert Van Grieken tried to find work as a carpenter. He went to the Labour Office, but found little help there. He asked about unemployment benefit but was told he would have to go and work on the Polders, repairing the damage the Germans had done. If he was made redundant, he might qualify.

Van Grieken felt he had had enough of general labouring during the previous five years. He wanted to be a carpenter, as he had started out. He was fortunate he could support himself while he looked for work. In accordance with his contract of employment with the Germans they had remitted to his home a proportion of his wages and his father had saved this money for him. It kept him going while he searched for a reasonable job. He was fortunate in finding a temporary job in a boat yard but this finished after a few weeks and he was no nearer finding permanent employment in his chosen trade.

Eventually he decided to try a contact he had made in Guernsey. While working at the Royal Hotel he had made some enquiries and had been in touch with a Mr. G. Rouillard, a carpenter and builder. Gilbert wrote to Mr. Rouillard to ask if there was any work as a carpenter to be had in Guernsey as conditions in Holland were so bad. He was delighted to have a reply telling him there was a job waiting for him in Guernsey and the necessary permit for him to take up the job had been obtained.

So, the former conscript forced labourer of the Organisation Todt, returned to Guernsey as a free man, in April 1946, and started to work for Mr. Rouillard, with whom he was to remain for the next seven years. Eventually he saved enough to be able to start up in business for himself and achieve the ambition he had set his sights on two decades earlier, before Hitler's armies intervened.

Eventually he married a Guernsey girl, who bore him two children, and became a British subject. In his heart he still sees himself as a Dutchman although he readily gives his loyalty to the community which adopted him and gave him sanctuary. He finds his native land much changed and feels a stranger there now. He is neither surprised nor dismayed that his children, born, raised and educated in Guernsey, have little interest in Holland. Their lives have been lived in Guernsey; their friends are there. For them the island is their native land.

The story of the journey Gilbert Van Grieken started out on nearly half a century ago has a happy ending but he will never forget the many of his countrymen, and others in Europe, whose lives were ruined by the evil that came out of Hitler's Third Reich. To him it is important that they are remembered so that the cry of the Little Peoples shall not go up to God in vain.